Items should be returned on or before the last date shown below. Items not already requested by other borrowers may be renewed in person, in writing or by telephone. To renew, please quote the number on the barcode label. To renew on line a PIN is required.
This can be requested at your local library.
Renew online @ **www.dublincitypubliclibraries.ie**
Fines charged for overdue items will include postage incurred in recovery. Damage to or loss of items will be charged to the borrower.

Date Due	Date Due	Date Due

Disclaimer

Walking and hillwalking are risk sports. The author and The Collins Press accept no responsibility for any injury, loss or inconvenience sustained by anyone using this guidebook.

To reduce the chance of break-in to parked cars, walkers are advised to place all valuables and belongings out of sight.

Advice to Readers

Every effort is made by our authors to ensure the accuracy of our guidebooks. However, changes can occur after a book has been printed, including changes to rights of way. If you notice discrepancies between this guidebook and the facts on the ground, please let us know, either by email to enquiries@collinspress.ie or by post to The Collins Press, West Link Park, Doughcloyne, Wilton, Cork, T12 N5EF, Ireland.

Acknowledgements

There are several people whose encouragement, participation and support were invaluable during the making of this guidebook, and to whom I owe a huge debt of gratitude. In particular, I would like to thank my wife Una, for the proofreading, love and support. Thanks also to all in The Collins Press for the continued support in my work, and for your expertise as always. And finally, thanks to Gudmund, Ray C., Derek, Gerry, Steven F., Steve B. and Una who have accompanied me on some of the walks; and also to Mairead of The Mourne Lodge, and Paul and Peter of Riverway House for your kind hospitality and welcome.

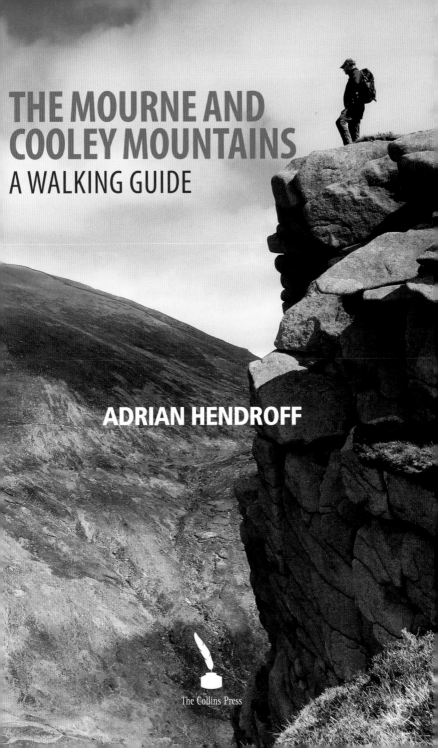

THE MOURNE AND COOLEY MOUNTAINS
A WALKING GUIDE

ADRIAN HENDROFF

The Collins Press

First published in 2018 by
The Collins Press
West Link Park
Doughcloyne
Wilton
Cork
T12 N5EF
Ireland

A CIP record for this book is available from the British Library.

Paperback ISBN: 978-1-84889-346-7

Design and typesetting by Fairways Design
Typeset in Myriad Pro
Printed in Poland by Białostockie Zakłady Graficzne SA

Photograph on page 1: Ben Crom across the Ben Crom Reservoir, with Slieve Bearnagh to the right.

Contents

Quick-Reference Route Table

No.	Route	Category
1	Slieve Croob	Hillwalk and mountain road
2	Millstone Mountain and Slieve Donard via Donard Forest	Hillwalk and forest trail
3	Chimney Rock Mountain from Bloody Bridge	Hillwalk and mountain trail
4	Slievenaglogh (N) to Slieve Commedagh via Hare's Gap	Hillwalk and mountain trail
5	Slieve Meelmore, Slieve Meelbeg and Slieve Loughshannagh	Hillwalk, mountain, reservoir and road trail
6	Slieve Bearnagh	
	Normal route	Hillwalk, mountain trail and optional scrambles
	South-east spur	Hillwalk, mountain trail and optional scrambles
7	Slieve Binnian and Blue Lough from Carrick Little	Hillwalk, mountain trail and optional scrambles
8	Rocky Mountain and Annalong Valley	Hillwalk, mountain and road trail
9	Slievelamagan, Cove Mountain, Slieve Beg and the Reservoir Trail	Hillwalk and reservoir trail
10	Moolieve, Wee Binnian and Slieve Binnian	Hillwalk, reservoir trail and optional scrambles
11	Slievenaglogh (S), Lough Shannagh, Carn Mountain and Slieve Muck	Hillwalk, scramble and mountain trai
12	Ben Crom and Doan	Hillwalk, mountain and reservoir trail
13	The Mourne Seven Sevens	Hillwalk, mountain trail and optional scrambles
14	The Mourne Wall Challenge	
	From Carrick Little or Silent Valley	Hillwalk and optional scrambles
	From Meelmore Lodge	Hillwalk and optional scrambles
15	Spelga, Spaltha, Butter Mountain and Slievenamuck	Hillwalk, mountain and road trail
16	Hen Mountain, Cock Mountain and Pigeon Rock Mountain	Hillwalk and mountain trail
17	Rocky Mountain, Tornamrock, Pierces Castle and Tievedockaragh	Hillwalk and mountain trail
18	Slievemoughanmore, Eagle Mountain and Shanlieve	
	From Community Centre	Hillwalk, mountain trail and road trail
	From top of Sandy Brae Road	Hillwalk and mountain trail
19	Cloghmore Stone, Slievemeen and Slievemartin	Hillwalk, mountain and forest trail
20	Annaloughan Forest Loop	Forest and road trail
21	Barnavave Loop from Carlingford	Hillwalk, mountain and road trail
22	Slieve Foye Forest and Ridge Walk	Hillwalk and forest trail
23	The Eagles Rock to The Foxes Rock from Greer's Quay	Hillwalk and road trail
24	The Hills and Forest of Ravensdale	Hillwalk, forest and road trail
25	Anglesey Mountain, Clermont and Flagstaff	Hillwalk, forest and road trail
26	Slieve Gullion	Hillwalk, mountain and road trail

Grade	Distance	Ascent	Time	Footwear	Page
2	9.5km	400m	3–4 hours	Boots	19
4	10km	870m	4–5 hours	Boots	27
3	8.5km	650m	3¼–4	Boots	33
3	12.5km	640m	4¼–5¼ hours	Boots	37
3	12km	735m	4¼–5¼ hours	Boots	42
4	8.5km	540m	3–4 hours	Boots	47
3	9.5km	540m	3½–4½	Boots	47
4	10km	605m	3½–4½ hours	Boots	52
3	15.5km	435m	5–6 hours	Boots	57
4	17.5km	775m	6–7 hours	Boots	64
4	11km	715m	4–5 hours	Boots	69
4	15km	790m	5¼–6¼ hours	Boots	75
4	17km	610m	5½–6½ hours	Boots	81
5	33km	2,660m	13–15 hours	Boots	88
5	33.5km	2,860m	14–16 hours	Boots	94
5	40.5km	3,080m	15–17 hours	Boots	94
2	6km	270m	2–2½ hours	Boots	103
3	10.5km	580m	3½–4½ hours	Boots	107
3	8.5km	485m	3–3¾ hours	Boots	112
3	14km	710m	4¾–5¾ hours	Boots	117
3	10.5km	660m	3½–4½ hours	Boots	117
3	9km	510m	3–4 hours	Boots	122
1	8.5km	230m	2½–3¼ hours	Runners	129
2	8.5km	350m	2¾–3½ hours	Boot/Runners	133
3	10.5km	585m	4–5 hours	Boots	137
3	11.5km	655m	4–5 hours	Boots	142
3	16km	565m	5–6 hours	Boots	147
3	12km	480m	3¾–4¾ hours	Boots	151
3	14.5km	440m	4½–5½ hours	Boots	156

Route Location Map

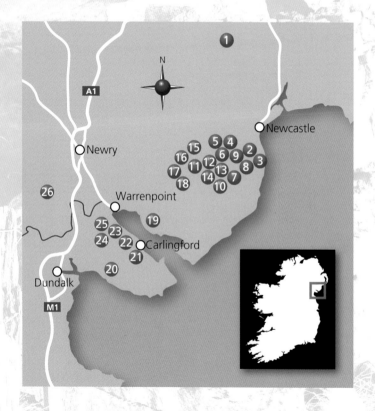

Using This Book

Maps

The maps in this guidebook are approximate representations of the routes only. For all routes in this guidebook, the use of detailed maps is imperative. All maps listed below are Ordnance Survey of Northern Ireland (OSNI) and Ordnance Survey Ireland (OSi) *Discovery* Series. Laminated versions are recommended for durability in wind and rain. Note that 1:50,000 OSi maps do not show cliffs, crags, boulder fields or areas of scree. Also, forestry, tracks and waymarked trails may change from time to time, so it is useful to get the latest edition.

The following maps are required for this guidebook:

- **OOSNI 1:25,000 *The Mournes Activity Map:*** Routes 1–19
- **OSNI 1:50,000 Sheet 29:** Routes 2–19 and 22–26
- **OSi 1:50,000 Sheet 36:** Routes 19–25

All maps may be purchased from most outdoor shops or online from: www.osi.ie or www.ordnancesurvey.co.uk

Grid References

Grid references (e.g. **J 357**98 **276**89) provided in this book should help you plan a route and upload it to your GPS or to use your GPS to check a grid reference on the mountain. Set your GPS to use the Irish Grid (IG). Note that GPS units are precise to five digits, whereas a three-digit precision will usually suffice using a map and compass, and hence these are outlined in **bold**.

Walking Times

Walking times in this book are calculated based on individual speeds of 3 to 4km per hour. One minute has also been added for every 10m of ascent, so for example for a height gain of 300m, 30 minutes will be added to the total walking time. E.g. a 6km route with a total of 300m ascent will take 2 to 2½ hours. In some routes, time has also been added to compensate for the difficulty of terrain, for example Slieve Bearnagh (Route 6) and Slieve Foye (Route 22).

Note that the 'Time' stated in the routes of this guidebook does not include the additional time required for stops, lunch, water intake and photography.

Metric and imperial units are given for road approaches (as some vehicles may be still using miles and road signs in Northern Ireland use imperial measurements), total distance, total ascent and mountain heights. However, walking distances are given in metric to conform to OSNI and OSi maps.

Walk Grades

Walks in this book are graded 1 to 5 based on *level of difficulty*, with 1 being the easiest and 5 the hardest. None of the routes involves any technical mountaineering or rock climbing. However, note that in winter under snow and ice conditions, all Grade 4 and 5 routes become a serious mountaineering venture requiring the use of winter mountaineering skills, crampons and ice axes. All routes with the exception of Grade 1 walks require three- to four-season hillwalking boots.

Grade 1:   Suited for beginners or families with children, these routes are on well-graded or constructed paths with good and firm underfoot conditions. There are little to no navigational difficulties as the routes are generally easy or signposted throughout. Grade 1 routes involve up to around 250m of total vertical ascent.

Grade 2:   Suited for beginners with some hillwalking experience, these routes are generally on formal paths or well-graded, constructed paths with good underfoot conditions. However, there may be some sections of open countryside or slightly rougher ground. The routes are generally signposted, but there may be sections with no signs and require basic navigational skills. Grade 2 routes involve up to 400m of total vertical ascent.

Grade 3:   Previous hillwalking experience is required. There may be some formal and signposted paths but generally these routes involve informal paths and rougher ground on open mountainside. There may be some sections of rocky and uneven ground, and small sections of cliffs and moderately steep ground. As they are generally not signed, good navigational skills in all weather conditions are required. Grade 3 routes involve from 400m to 750m of total vertical ascent.

Grade 4:   Suited for those with solid hillwalking experience. Paths are generally informal and underfoot conditions are rough. There may be prolonged sections of rocky and uneven ground.

Solid mountain navigation skills are required to cope with all weather conditions. The ability to deal with hazards such as cliffs, small sections of scree and steep ground is required. Some (optional) basic scrambling skills are also required. Grade 4 routes involve from 500m to 900m of total vertical ascent.

Grade 5:   This is the same as Grade 4, except it involves walking distances of around 40km and up to 3,000m of total vertical ascent. Grade 5 routes are highly strenuous and physically demanding, and best suited for endurance or challenge hillwalkers.

Access

All land in Ireland is owned privately or by the State (Republic of Ireland) or the Crown (Northern Ireland) with no legal right of entry to the land. When you hear the term 'commonage' it implies that the private property is held in common by a number of joint owners.

Access to upland and mountain areas has traditionally been granted out of the goodwill, permission and discretion of the landowners. It is normally good practice to strike up a friendly conversation with a farmer or landowner, and if there is any doubt about access, to ask them. If you are asked to leave, please do so politely and without argument or aggravating the situation.

Note also the provisions of the Occupiers Liability Act 1995 contain a definition that reduces the landowner's duty of care to hillwalkers. This act contains a category of 'recreational users' who, when they enter farmland, are responsible for their own safety. This has significantly reduced the possibility of successful legal claims against landowners by hillwalkers.

Always use gates and stiles where available. If a gate is closed, close it after entering. If it is open, leave it open. If you cannot open a closed gate to enter, go over at its hinge with care. Take care not to damage any gates, stiles or fences.

When parking, be considerate not to block any gates, farm access lanes or forest entrances as local residents, farm machinery and emergency services may need access at all times.

With the exception of public parks, note that landowners generally do not approve of dogs being brought on their property, and this includes their land on the open hillside. If you insist, ask the landowner's permission and keep your dogs on a leash.

Mountain Safety

1. Get a detailed weather forecast. The best mountain weather website for the Mournes and Slieve Gullion is www.metoffice.gov.uk. For all other areas, use www.met.ie, www.mountain-forecast.com or www. yr.no. There is also the Met Éireann Weatherdial service on 1550 123 853 (if calling from the Republic of Ireland) or 0906 753 5577 (if calling from the UK/Northern Ireland) that provides a detailed five-day weather forecast for Ulster.

2. There is a temperature drop of 2 to 3ºC for every 300m of ascent. If it is a pleasant morning at sea level it could be cold on the summit of Slieve Donard. The wind is around 25 per cent stronger at 500m than at sea level. Wind velocities at a col are higher and wind effects could be strong on an exposed ridge.

3. In case of emergency call 999/112 and ask for 'Mountain Rescue'. Before dialling, it helps to be ready to give a grid location of your position.

4. Keep well away from cliff edges. Be cautious of wet or slippery rock and holes in the ground on vegetated slopes. Take your time traversing a boulder field, descending a scree slope and during scrambling.

5. Rivers, marked as 'thick' blue lines on OSi maps, can sometimes be little streams. Similarly, some streams, marked as 'thin' blue lines, can be wide rivers in reality. Remember also that rivers or streams in flood are dangerous and water levels can rise very quickly after or during wet days. Always cross rivers with boots on – remove your socks to keep them dry, use a plastic liner inside your boots to cross, use a towel to dry your feet and boots after, and then put your dry socks back on. Avoid river crossings early in the day. If you cannot cross a river in spate, head upstream to increase your chances in crossing. Do not cross rivers at a bend, rather cross on a straight.

6. Ensure that you and your boots, clothing and equipment are up to the task, and know the limitations of each. Winter conditions involving snow and ice require specialised gear including winter boots, ice axes and crampons.

7. Be aware of the daylight hours over the time of year. Most accidents happen during descent or near the end of the day. Carry enough emergency equipment (e.g. a head torch, survival shelter and spare batteries) should an injury occur and you need to stop moving.

8.   It is recommended not to walk alone, except in areas where there are other people around. Leave word with someone responsible.

9.   Do not leave any valuables in cars. Keep all things in the boot and out of sight to avoid unwanted attention.

10. Carry a fully charged mobile phone, but keep it well away from the compass as its needle gets affected by metal. Note that the compass needle can also be affected by GPS units, phone cases or gloves with magnetic closing flaps, and any outdoor jackets with magnets tucked away in the folds of the garment.

11. Do not solely rely on the use of GPS. Map and compass skills are imperative.

12. Landowners, especially farmers, move their livestock such as cattle from field to field, and up to higher ground, especially in the summer. Be wary of bulls in fields and cows that are protecting newborn calves. Avoid crossing such fields and go another way. If you find yourself in a field of suddenly wary cattle, do not panic: move away calmly, without making any sudden noises. The cows may leave you alone if they think you pose no threat.

Useful Contacts

Access and Training Mountaineering Ireland, the representative body for walkers and climbers in Ireland, works to secure continued access and to provide walkers and climbers the opportunity to improve their skills. Tel: +353 (0)1 6251115; www.mountaineering.ie

Hillwalking Resource www.mountainviews.ie is a great hillwalking resource and provides mountain lists, comments and information. Also, check out these local websites for Northern Ireland and the Mourne Mountains: www.walkni.com and www.enjoythemournes.com

Tourist Information A useful website on accommodation and things to do in Northern Ireland is discovernorthernireland.com. For the Cooley Peninsula, the tourist office at Carlingford is full of useful information: Carlingford tourist office, Cooley Peninsula Tourism, Address: Old Railway Station, Carlingford, County Louth, Ireland. Tel: +353 (0) 42 9373033. Website: www.carlingfordandcooleypeninsula.ie. Finally, specific information on the Ring of Gullion can be found at: www.ringofgullion.org

Transport By Bus For information on bus services to and from the area within Northern Ireland see www.translink.co.uk/Routes-and-Timetables/.

For information on bus services from the Republic of Ireland see, www. buseireann.ie. **By Train** Irish Rail provides a service from Dublin to Belfast, passing through main towns towards the west of the Mournes. Up-to-date timetables are available on www.irishrail.ie. **By Ferry** A ferry for foot passengers, cyclists, cars, vans and caravans provides transport from Greenore (County Louth) to Greencastle (County Down). Check sailing timetables at: https://carlingfordferry.com

Traffic The Northern Ireland Department for Infrastructure provides useful traffic updates, including roadworks and diversions, as well as a winter service and emergency news, see: www.trafficwatchni.com

Mourne Shuttle Service A 16-seat minibus provides a hillwalker service, including a bespoke pick-up and set-down in all regions of the Mournes. It includes stops at key walking start and finish points described in this book such as Meelmore Lodge, Donard Park, Bloody Bridge and Carrick Little: Tel: +44 (0)7516 412 076.

Cloughmore Stone near Rostrevor, with a section of Carlingford Lough visible to the left (Route 19).

Introduction: The Mournes

But for all that I found there I might as well be
Where the Mountains of Mourne sweep down to the sea.
– William Percy French (1854–1920)

The Mourne Mountains, the jewels of Northern Ireland that 'sweep down to the sea', hug the County Down coastline in a compact region designated as an Area of Outstanding Natural Beauty (AONB). These are the mountains that inspired Belfast-born novelist C.S. Lewis to create his magical land of Narnia. Less than an hour's drive from Belfast and around two hours by car from Dublin, these are the peaks of Mourne, formed millions of years ago by fire and ice.

These peaks are the highest and most dramatic mountain range in Northern Ireland, a circular cluster of majestic granite tops, some sharp and rugged, others more rounded domes, dominating the Mourne landscape in almost every direction. Some of the rocky summits are even crowned by an exquisite collection of granite tors of various shapes and sizes. In fact, granite is everywhere – granite rocks are strewn around deep valleys, granite boulders dot riverbanks, granite buttresses line the crags, and a granite wall links its summits.

Before they were known as the Mournes, these mountains were called *Na Beanna Bóirche*, or 'the hills of Boirche'. Boirche, a 250 AD Celtic chieftain, was recognised as 'the cow herd to the High King of Ulster', a name bestowed on him based on the number of cattle he owned, a measure of wealth in those days. The name 'Mourne', however, was only derived in later years, evolving from a Gaelic clan called *Múghdorna*.

In his book, *In Search of Ireland*, H.V. Morton speaks of the mountains of Mourne being different from the hills of the west of Ireland, yet, he writes, '… are linked to all these by that unearthly quality of the Irish landscape which I can describe only as something half of this world and half in the next'. The Mourne landscape is a chapter in time, not at the beginning or the end, but still in transit, evolving at nature's geological pace that is completely oblivious to humans.

Around 420 million years ago during the Silurian era, before the existence of Ireland, the Mourne area was covered by an immense ocean called the Iapetus. At the very bottom of this ocean were sand, silt and mud. These were repeatedly compressed over millions of years by the weight of younger rocks and baked by intense heat until they were turned into Silurian shales. Today, these shales are the oldest rocks found in the Mournes and are located north of Slieve Croob, between Moneyscalp and Hare's Gap, and from the foothills of Slieve Binnian to the sea.

Next, roughly 400 million years ago, the ancient continents started to collide, making it a time of unprecedented volcanic activity across the earth. Molten rock bubbled up underneath multiple layers of shales, without a chance of escaping through the surface. The rock later cooled, forming extensive domes of hard, igneous rock known today as granite. Such periods of extreme heat and cold continued until around 56 million years ago, culminating in a series of at least half a dozen ice ages that ended 10,000 years ago. The ice scraped, ground and carved the rocks with ferocious intensity and shaped the landscape to reveal the mountains and valleys that grace the Mournes today.

Long after the mountains were formed, Mesolithic hunters, Neolithic farmers and Bronze Age settlers cut their way inland through the great forests between 5000 and 500 BC. These pagan communities had a strong reverence for high places, evident from the remnants of ancient cairns, stone structures and burial chambers they built on some of the summits. However, it was not until the dawn of Christianity that the boundaries of the kingdom of Mourne became defined. Here, it was said that St Patrick threw his sandal between the streams of Srupatrick and Cassy Water – it flew twelve Irish miles, marking the 'Twelve Miles of Mourne'. Other saints are also associated with the Mourne area, for example St Domangard is linked with Slieve Donard, building an oratory on its summit, and St Bronagh is tied to the Rostrevor area, with a ruined church dedicated to her near the village.

In medieval Ireland around the fifteenth and sixteenth centuries, the kingdom of Mourne fell under the rule of the wealthy Magennis clan, whose chiefs were inaugurated at a coronation stone on the Bridle Loaning above Warrenpoint. This lasted until the Rebellion of 1641, when Magennis lands were taken over by Anglo-Norman settlers, who soon populated all the towns and villages dotted across the Mourne foothills.

The Mourne Mountains are bounded by the towns of Hilltown and Newcastle to the north, and Rostrevor and Kilkeel to the south. A road runs along the coast from Rostrevor to Newcastle via Kilkeel; another runs inland from Hilltown to Newcastle; and two more cut through the mountains from Kilkeel to Hilltown, and Rostrevor to Hilltown respectively. The mountains are highly accessible, all interlinked by an unrivalled network of tracks and paths. They also boast one of the most remarkable structural feats: the 35km (22-mile) Mourne Wall, built by men as tough as nails over eighteen long years between 1904 and 1922.

The routes in this guidebook encompass Slieve Croob and two distinct upland areas in the Mournes. The first covers the bigger and higher peaks of the Eastern Mournes, including 23 summits in total, of which thirteen rise over 600m or 2,000ft. A lesser-used circuit to the highest point in Northern Ireland (Slieve Donard) is also described, as well as two classic mountain challenge walks in the area, one of which traces the course of the mighty Mourne Wall. Some summits also include an optional scramble (or two) to the top of granite tors or rocky outcrops. The second area covers the sixteen lower peaks of the Western Mournes, which extend from a group of rounded hills to the north of Spelga Dam, to the twin peaks of Slievemeen and Slievemartin above the woods of Rostrevor.

It is hoped that this guidebook will unlock the doors for many of you to begin exploring this fascinating mountain kingdom of County Down and Northern Ireland. For the more experienced, perhaps some walks will provide fresh ideas or a different perspective as the route descriptions include snippets on the flora, fauna, heritage, history, geology and folklore of each area. Finally, for the challenge walkers or more ambitious amongst you, I have no doubt you will relish the epic Mourne Seven Sevens or Mourne Wall challenge, or perhaps combine the high-level routes described in this book to form a longer and more entertaining variation.

Happy hiking the mountains that sweep down to the sea!

The stunning view towards Slieve Binnian and Silent Valley Reservoir from the rocky summit of Doan (Route 12).

Slieve Croob

A straightforward walk
to enjoy one of the most
expansive views in the
kingdom of Mourne.

Grade:	2
Distance:	9.5km (6 miles)
Ascent:	400m (1,312ft)
Time:	3–4 hours
Map:	OSNI 1:25,000 *The Mournes Activity Map*

Start/finish: Large car park at the church in Finnis/Massford (grid ref: **J 284**₆₉ **476**₉₈). Alternative car park at Dree Hill (grid ref: **J 300**₄₈ **452**₅₂).

Getting there: From Newry, head north-east, following the A25 towards Rathfriland. From there, take the B7 to Moneyslane and continue in the direction of Dromara for around 9.5km (6 miles) to reach the hamlet of Finnis/Massford. The church is on the right, just before the Dree Hill junction. If parking at the alternative car park at Dree Hill, turn right at the junction after the church. Ignore a junction on the left and continue uphill for around 3.3km (2 miles) to reach Dree Hill car park.

Slieve Croob is an outlier of the Mournes and a solitary peak tucked between the village of Dromara and Castlewellan town. It is part of the rugged Dromara landscape, whose ancient bedrock was formed even before the dinosaurs roamed the earth. Craggy uplands, rolling drumlin hills, little oval hills, tiny ridges and fertile pastures – all characteristics of the expansive landscape that can be fully appreciated from Slieve Croob.

The River Lagan begins as a tiny stream from its source near the summit of Slieve Croob, the start of its 73km (45-mile) journey towards Belfast. At 534m/1752ft,

Signboard at the wall at the start of the Slieve Croob Permissive Path at Pass Loaning.

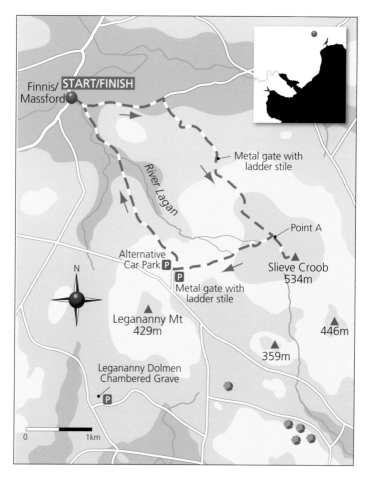

Slieve Croob (*Sliabh Crúb*, 'mountain of the hoof') is the highest peak in the Dromara hills. Its summit boasts one of the finest panoramas of mountain, sea and plains in the kingdom of Mourne, with views as far and wide as the Isle of Man and the Mull of Kintyre across the Irish Sea. The rugged Dromara hills are some 380 million years old, much older than their higher cousins to the south, the Mourne Mountains.

In the height of summer, the foothills of Slieve Croob are vividly coloured by yellow gorse, pink heather and purple moor grass. Its extensive field system is bordered by drystone walls, where stoats dart from dark cavities and hedges of furze, hawthorn and holly. Skylarks, meadow pipits, thrushes and starlings roam the air over the grasslands, which extend to the sand dunes of Murlough and Dundrum Bay.

The tarmac road just after Point A, with the masts on Slieve Croob's summit slopes ahead.

There was once a huge burial cairn on the summit in ancient times. In *A Topographical Dictionary of Ireland Volume 1, 1837*, Lewis wrote: 'among the antiquities are two remarkable Cairns; one of them on the summit of Slieve Croob, measuring 80 yards around the base and 50 on the top, and forming the largest monument of the kind in the country'. This enormous cairn was rearranged at a later date to form a dozen smaller cairns, giving it its local name of the 'Twelve Cairns'. Now all that remains are some cairn shelters around a trig point.

This route begins and ends in the hamlet of Finnis/Massford, on the north-western slopes of Slieve Croob near Dromara. It takes in the summit of Slieve Croob in a clockwise fashion: by way of a quiet country lane, followed by a mountain access path across the rugged slopes of Monahoora to reach the summit, before descending along the 'transmitter' track to the alternative car park at the top of Dree Hill Road. The final stretch is downhill on tarmac back to Finnis/Massford.

Route Description

Exit the church car park, turn right and walk a short distance to reach the Dree Hill junction. Turn right there onto Dree Hill road. After around 200m, turn left and continue along Drin Road for around 1.2km to reach a set of junctions (grid ref: J **298**77 **477**25) with a farm building on the right.

Leave the road and turn right here onto Pass Loaning. There is a Slieve Croob Permissive Path signboard on the wall with a note to remind visitors not to bring dogs onto the mountain because of livestock.

Follow the concrete road to pass a bungalow on the right. The road is soon flanked by hedges before passing another bungalow on the left. Beyond a bend at some farm buildings soon after, the road begins to go gradually uphill. The road is flanked with a vast cobweb of stone-walled fields of green pastures and sheep.

Extensive views of the flat, surrounding countryside now beckon to the left. Soon pass a copse of trees with a ruined building on the left, followed by a sheep's pen with a 'No Parking' sign before reaching a metal gate with a ladder stile (grid ref: **J 306**72 **468**25).

A snow-capped Slieve Donard seen from the summit of Slieve Croob.

Follow a broad, muddy track beyond the stile to reach a fork. A Yellow Man sign on a tree marks the way forward. Continue ahead along a broad, grassy track, following the signposts uphill.

As height is gained, much of the view behind you and to your left is a wide stretch of flat countryside dominated by a patchwork of green fields, interrupted only by the white blades of wind turbines and the grey buildings of Dromara village.

The signposts lead uphill on a grassy slope along an indistinct path to reach a stile in the fence (grid ref: **J 311**50 **462**50). After a boggy stretch beyond the stile, some communication masts – a good landmark to aim for – come into view on the hilltop ahead.

Keep following the signposts to reach another stile at a fence. A distinct path soon gives way to rough and boggy terrain. The open hillside here is known as Monahoora and is home to the skylark. Its continuous stream of song is the quintessential sound of early summer in these hills. Meadow pipits, with their tuneful *pheet pheet* notes, can also be heard. Kestrels, recognised by their fanned tail, hover in updrafts. Large buzzards and red kites can also be seen on occasion.

Keep an eye out for those birds as you persevere across the rough terrain. Aim for the masts and before long you will arrive at a tarmac road at a bend (Point A). Continue uphill on the transmitter road toward the masts until it forks. Veer right at the fork, soon reaching an information board.

Shortly, as the road takes a bend, a sudden and stupendous view of the Mourne Mountains opens up to the right (south). The full stretch of the Mournes can be appreciated from here, but continue, as the view is even better from the top!

The view south-east from the trig pillar and burial cairn on the summit of Slieve Croob.

The road ends just below some masts. Now, step over a wooden stile and follow an obvious path to reach the summit of Slieve Croob, marked by a trig pillar and cairns (grid ref: **J 318**$_{60}$ **453**$_{77}$).

The view is all-encompassing and stretches as far as the rolling Sperrins to the west, Lough Neagh to the north-west and Agnew's Hill to the north. The Black Mountains of Belfast can also be made out to the north, as can the shoreline of Dundrum Bay and the dunes of Murlough to the south-east. But the landmark that dominates the eye is the towering range of the High Mournes, which rises behind the extensive 'basket of eggs' drumlin landscape to the south.

Retrace steps from the summit back to Point A. From here, stay on the transmitter road and follow it downhill to reach Dree Hill car park. The road provides an easy way off the mountain, whose slopes are dominated by thick heather and tufted mat-grass. In the summer, the fluffy seed heads of cotton grass quiver in wet, peaty areas.

At the end of the road, use a swinging metal gate next to the main gate into Dree Hill car park. If you have not parked here, exit the car park and turn right onto Dree Hill Road and follow it back to Finnis/Massford.

Legananny Dolmen

Getting there: From the church car park at Finnis/Massford, turn left back on the B7 towards Moneyslane. After 300m, leave the B7, and turn left into Carrigagh Road. Continue for around 2km (1¼ miles) to reach Finnis crossroads. Continue straight ahead at the crossroads and after 1km (0.6 mile), turn left into Legananny Road. Follow the winding road for around 2.3km (1½ miles), then turn left again onto the narrow Dolmen Road. The dolmen parking is at a lay-by (grid ref: **J 289**$_{15}$ **432**$_{87}$) around 150m up the road. Access to the dolmen is on a footpath along a lane near a farm bungalow from the car park.

Legananny Dolmen (*Liagán Áine*, 'pillar stone of Anya') dates back to the Neolithic period (2500–2000 BC) and is worth a visit. The word 'dolmen' is from the Breton word *tolmen* meaning 'stone table'. Anya was the mother goddess lover of the legendary warrior Fionn MacCumhaill in Irish mythology. The dolmen, a single burial chamber tomb, is characterised by three tall upright stones supporting a massive, sloping capstone.

Legananny Dolmen.

The Eastern 'High' Mournes

This group of peaks is in a compact area stretching between Newcastle in the north, Kilkeel to the south, and bordered by the B27 and Slievenaman Road to its west. Thirteen of the peaks rise to over 600m (2,000ft), dominating the Mourne landscape in every direction. One mountain towers head and shoulders above the rest: Slieve Donard, the highest in County Down and Northern Ireland.

The Eastern 'High' Mournes are steep and shapely, and some have craggy tors. Rocky crags, pinnacles, buttresses and gullies also feature amongst the peaks. These granite tops are also separated by long U-shaped valleys carved by glaciers during the ice age over 12,000 years ago. The area also receives some of the highest rainfall in Northern Ireland. The mountains of the High Mournes act as a water-catchment area bounded by the great Mourne Wall, which runs along a string of summits for a distance of about 35km (22 miles). A network of rivers also tumbles down fiercely from the steep mountainside, emanating from nearly every corner of this compact range, like arteries from the heart. Conifer and broadleaved woodland also envelope the hillside extensively to the north and north-east, and more patchily to the south and south-east.

The table below lists the 23 peaks of the Eastern 'High' Mournes featured in this guidebook, in order of height. Note that all heights are based on the OSNI 1:25,000 *The Mournes Activity Map*.

Mountain Name	Height	Route
Slieve Donard	853m/2,799ft (Trig Pillar)	2, 13, 14
Slieve Commedagh	765m/2,510ft	4, 13, 14
Slieve Binnian	747m/2,451ft	7, 13, 14
Slieve Bearnagh	739m/2,425ft	6, 13, 14
Slieve Meelbeg	708m/2,323ft	5, 13, 14
Slievelamagan	704m/2,310ft	9, 13
Slieve Meelmore	680m/2,231ft	5, 13, 14
Slieve Binnian North Tor	678m/2,224ft	7, 10, 13
Slieve Muck	674m/2,211ft	11, 13
Chimney Rock Mountain	656m/2,152ft	3
Cove Mountain	655m/2,149ft	9, 13
Slieve Corragh	640m/2,100ft	4, 14
Slieve Loughshannagh	619m/2,031ft	5, 14
Doan	594m/1,949ft	12
Slieve Beg	590m/1,936ft	9, 13

Mountain Name	Height	Route
Carn Mountain	588m/1,929ft	11, 14
Slievenaglogh (N)	586m/1,923ft	4, 13
Ben Crom	526m/1,726ft	12
Rocky Mountain	525m/1,722ft	8, 14
Millstone Mountain	460m/1,509ft	2
Wee Binnian	460m/1,509ft	10, 14
Slievenaglogh (S)	445m/1,460ft	11, 14
Moolieve	332m/1,089ft	10, 14

On the path leading down to the Glen River. Dundrum Bay can be seen to the left (Route 2).

Millstone Mountain and Slieve Donard via Donard Forest

Enjoy a lesser-known route to the top of Northern Ireland.

Grade:	4
Distance:	10km (6¼ miles)
Ascent:	870m (2,854 ft)
Time:	4–5 hours
Map:	OSNI 1:25,000 *The Mournes Activity Map* or OSNI 1:50,000 Sheet 29

Start/Finish: Donard Park main car park (grid ref: **374**42 **305**70).

Getting there: If approaching from Kilkeel/Annalong/Bloody Bridge (A2) along Kilkeel Road, follow signs for Donard car park before reaching Newcastle. If approaching from Bryansford (B180)/Dundrum (A2), head into Newcastle and aim for the coast road to Bloody Bridge/Annalong/Kilkeel (A2). Follow signs for Donard car park before reaching the coast road.

There is nowhere higher in the Mournes nor, indeed, Northern Ireland than the summit of Slieve Donard, thus making it a unique vantage point for appreciating views far and wide, including the iconic Mourne Wall and all the great peaks in the area.

In ancient times, the mountain was known as *Sliabh Slainge*, named after Slanga, a Partholan prince of Grecian origin who came to these shores after the battle of Troy. Its summit cairn came to be known as 'Slainge's Cairn', as it was reputedly his final resting place, known today as the Great Carn. And so it was that the mountain was named after him.

Waterfall at Donard Bridge.

27

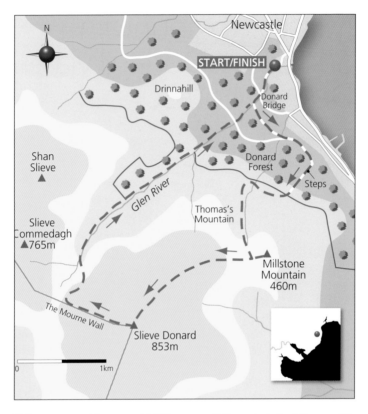

This name stood for around 2,000 years until the arrival of a follower of St Patrick's, St Domangard, in the fifth century. Domangard, like other great Irish saints, found heavenly solace on such lofty heights, and he built an oratory on the summit. The stones of the Great Carn may have once been part of the saint's oratory and even his passage grave. The mountain soon became known and accepted as *Sliabh Domangard*, and now Donard, a corruption of his name.

The route begins from the popular Donard Park in the busy seaside town of Newcastle, which derives its name from a tower house built by Felix Magenis in 1588 at the mouth of the Shimna River. As the house was erected on the site of an old castle, it became known as the 'New Castle'. The Annesley family, known for their contribution to the development of Castlewellan, were also influential in transforming Newcastle from a fishermen's village into a thriving seaside resort.

The usual and most popular route to the summit is an out-and-back from Donard Park via Donard Forest, then along the Glen River trail to the col

Looking north from the Lesser Carn toward Dundrum Bay, from near the summit of Slieve Donard.

below Slieve Donard, and from there following the Mourne Wall steeply to the top. However, the route in this book is an elegant circuit, approaching Slieve Donard from its north-eastern spur and returning by way of the Glen River trail. The north-eastern spur is approached via a section of the Granite Trail, a waymarked route that links a number of sites in the area associated with the granite industry of the late eighteenth century. This industry thrived up to the Second World War, when Mourne granite was dressed and supplied as kerbs and cobblestones for the booming cities of industrial Britain. In recent times, the same granite was used in the 9/11 British Memorial Garden (New York), Hans Christian Andersen statue in Central Park (New York), Parliament Buildings in Stormont (Belfast) and the 'Silence' Water Feature at the Connaught Hotel (London).

Route Description

Take the gravel track at the southern end of the main car park (if in doubt, it is toward the overspill car park). The track, bordered by a green fence, meanders alongside the sports pitches and park grounds to reach Donard Wood.

Enter the woods and ascend the leafy slopes. The Glen River runs nearby to the left, and though it is hidden from view, the gushing flow of water can be heard. A path leads uphill through tangled woods of beech, birch, oak and pine. Chestnut, rowan, holly and ivy trees make up the rest of the greenery.

29

Looking towards Slieve Commedagh from the western slopes of Slieve Donard in winter.

The lower confines of the riverbed are lined with ancient Silurian rock, whose scarred and rough surface contrasts with the grainy texture of the granite which replaces it further upstream.

A row of servants' quarters once led to the two-storey Donard Lodge, which was built in 1831 by the 3rd Earl, William Annesley. Today, patches of cobblestones are all that remain after the lodge was demolished in 1966, having been damaged in the Second World War.

Avoid the tree roots, which can be a hazard on a wet day, and continue uphill to reach Donard Bridge, a granite arch built in 1835. Go left and cross the bridge, stopping only to admire the waterfall tumbling down a rocky shelf on the right. It is common to see butterflies here such as the silver-washed fritillary, green hairstreak and holly blue.

Next, veer right onto a cobbled path immediately after the bridge. The Glen River now flows to your right. Leave the cobbled path at a fork and head left onto a surfaced forest track beyond a metal barrier. The track climbs uphill through the woods to soon pass an arched granite enclosure with the year 1842 inscribed on a stone plaque. Ignore two forest tracks on the right after the granite enclosure and keep to the main track as it contours along forested slopes.

After crossing a small stream, the main track meets another track leading uphill on the right. Ignore this and continue until reaching the Granite Trail information board at the base of a flight of steps leading steeply uphill, also on the right. There was once a funicular railway here, which rattled down from old quarries above to King Street, south of Newcastle, near the sea. This railway was named the Bogie Line after the iron trucks or bogies which transported the granite to be shipped from Newcastle. The original line, built by John Lynn in 1824, had cables attached to a pair of bogies on rails, with the weight of the fully loaded descending bogie assisting to haul up the empty one.

Turn right and ascend the steps. It is steep, but pause to look back at Dundrum Bay, visible through the trees as height is gained. Finally, reach a ladder stile and a wooden gate at a fence further uphill. The wooden Shoddy Hut, used as shelter by stoneworkers involved in building the Mourne Wall, sits nearby. Its name originated from pieces of granite, called 'shoddies', that remained after dressing stone. Each Shoddy Hut came complete with tools, bellows and furnace.

Cross the stile, then veer right onto a mainly earthen path running near the forest edge. The imposing mass of Millstone Mountain rises to the left as the path leads gently uphill to meet another wooden gate and stile. Enter the gate, then head left to reach the base of a large quarry below Thomas's Mountain. Take the eroded path to the right of a large zinc hut with a concrete base. Follow a fence on the left and descend to reach a rusted metal gate by a wall.

Go left here toward a small concrete hut and use an informal, earthen path leading uphill. After a moderately steep slope, arrive at a flat area above the quarry – an ideal place for a rest to appreciate the sprawling panorama from Dundrum Bay and back inland to Castlewellan.

The path turns grassy after this and runs to the right of a stream-filled gorge. Continue uphill to reach a flat, boggy area at a col, before veering left up a short rise to reach the small cairn marking Millstone Mountain. The views of the foothills, plains and the sea are even better from here.

Retrace steps to the col then head west on a grassy and heathery slope to reach a grassy shoulder. From here, the spur that rises south-west toward Slieve Donard may be appreciated.

Ascend the spur, taking into account the incline, which becomes steeper with height, and the increasingly rocky terrain. Negotiate some boulder fields with care higher upslope – you may need to get hands on rock in places but no serious scrambling is required. Soon, you reach a stone shelter and the Lesser Carn, which is possibly an ancient burial cairn.

The steepness finally relents soon before reaching the Great Carn and the trig pillar placed on top of a stone lookout tower, marking the summit of Slieve Donard (grid ref: **J 357**98 **276**89). At once the expansive view of mountains and the sea unfolds: Slieve Commedagh and Chimney Rock Mountain to the north-west and south-east; the range of peaks across the Annalong Valley as far south as Slieve Binnian; the jagged tors of Slieve Bearnagh in the distance. On a very clear day, even the distant profile of the Wicklow Mountains, the Galloway Hills of Scotland and the Isle of Man can be seen.

From the summit, keep the Mourne Wall to your left and with Slieve Commedagh in front of you, descend steeply to the col below. At the col, turn right before a ladder stile and walk towards a large cairn. Meet a path that descends into the Glen River Valley there, initially quite steeply down some granite steps, and soon passing some large boulders.

The icehouse seen across the Glen River.

Once down in the Upper Glen River Valley, cross a stream using stepping stones, then go right onto a path constructed of granite slabs. The descent is gradual, so take your time to appreciate the scenic valley, with the Glen River on the right, and imposing crags and scree-fringed slopes on either side.

Follow the path until it reaches Donard Wood, where it runs along the edge of the conifers. With the trees on your left, follow the earthen path, which is paved with granite slabs in places to prevent further erosion.

The river on the right is strewn with boulders; just before entering the woods, look out for an igloo-shaped icehouse on its opposite bank. Built in the nineteenth century, the structure was used to store food for the now-demolished Donard Lodge. The icehouse was purchased by the National Trust from the Annesleys in 1991, and later restored.

On reaching a broad U-shaped forest track, ignore it. Instead, pick out on a narrow path across the track, which descends steeply through the woods. Negotiate some large granite rock slabs and also be mindful of slippery tree roots, especially after rain.

The Glen River can be heard to your right. Soon, you reach another bridge and here continue to descend through the woods, still keeping the river to your right. Large slabs of granite rock can be seen in the riverbed along this section but underfoot conditions improve with height loss. The slope soon relents and turns into a stony track as you reach Donard Bridge once again.

Retrace your steps from here back to the start.

Chimney Rock Mountain from Bloody Bridge

A half-day's hike to one of the loveliest viewpoints in the Mournes. Visit an old quarry too.

Grade:	3
Distance:	8.5km (5¼ miles)
Ascent:	650m (2,133ft)
Time:	3¼–4 hours
Map:	OSNI 1:25,000 *The Mournes Activity Map* or OSNI 1:50,000 Sheet 29

Start/Finish: Bloody Bridge car park (grid ref: **J 388**₇₈ **270**₈₉).

Getting there: Bloody Bridge car park can be reached by driving north along Kilkeel Road (A2) for around 7km (4¼ miles) from Annalong, or south for just under 4km (2½ miles) from Newcastle. The car park gets quite busy, especially at public holidays or weekends.

The distinctive profile of Chimney Rock Mountain was commonly used in the past by Mourne fishermen as a landmark to steer them to their fishing grounds off the Glasdrumman coast. Its lower slopes can also be seen rising from Bloody Bridge, a well-known parking spot and access point to the High Mournes.

The original 'Bloody Bridge' lies a few hundred metres upstream from the present one, which crosses the coast road. Now wreathed in ivy, the old single-arch stone bridge is almost a forgotten antiquity. In his 1900 book *Official Guide to County Down and the Mourne Mountains* Robert Lloyd Praeger wrote that the old Bloody Bridge 'derives its gruesome name from the massacre of a number of protestants of Newry, including their minister, in the troubled year of 1641 at the instigation of Sir Conn Magennis'.

Today, the sins of the past are repeatedly washed when the river swells to a torrent during or after heavy rainfall. Bloody Bridge River is known as a 'spate river', changing its character at the whim of the weather. So, although the river carries little more than a trickle in dry conditions, things can quickly change. Note therefore that the river may be difficult to cross on wet days, and this route requires crossing it both at the start and end of the walk.

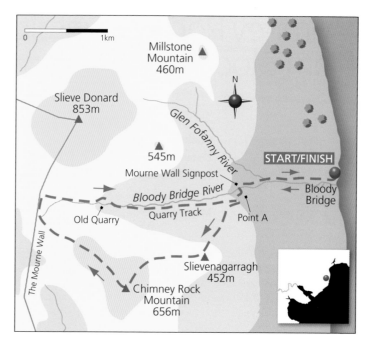

Route Description

Exit the car park near the public toilets at its southern end. Walk a few metres along the road in the direction of Annalong and cross the road to meet the start of the Bloody Bridge track. Enter a wooden gate beside a larger metal gate, followed by a wooden 'squeeze' stile shortly after.

A track runs to the right of the Bloody Bridge River. Follow the well-defined track, which is flanked by swathes of gorse and bracken. Bare granite rock overlays the track in places, matching the rocky character of the river, which is full of rock pools and tilted slabs of granite. Two pipelines also cross the river, carrying water from the Silent Valley to Belfast.

After around a kilometre from the road, cross a wooden bridge, then a stile and after another 350m, reach a Mourne Wall sign at a fork (grid ref: **J 377**06 **269**42). Veer left here onto a path leading down to the river. Cross the river onto a broad track on its opposite bank and continue to a metal gate. Ascend the concrete steps before the gate, which leads to a wooden ladder stile placed over a fence (Point A).

Climb over the stile, then turn right onto a broad track leading uphill. The track straightens after a bend and passes under the steep, grassy slopes of Slievenagarragh. Leave the track at any convenient point and go left uphill. After some rocky patches, arrive at a cairn marking the broad shoulder of Slievenagarragh.

34

Hillwalkers heading north-west along the spur on Chimney Rock Mountain, with Cove Mountain, Slievelamagan and Slieve Bearnagh in the background.

This is a good place for a rest before the final ascent of Chimney Rock Mountain. The blue sea sweeps across to the east, extending north towards Dundrum Bay before tracing an arc to St John's Point. The green southern confines of Donard Forest are also apparent, with the dunes of Murlough as a backdrop. Back inland, and to the north-west, the hulking mass of Slieve Donard towers skyward from the brown shoulder of Crossone.

When ready, head west, then later go south-west toward Chimney Rock Mountain. The slope is steep initially but finally relents as you approach the large cairn on its broad, rocky summit (grid ref: **J 364**₁₇ **257**₂₅).

Views of the sea and bay are even better from here, topped by an expanse of patchwork fields to the south and south-east beyond Spences Mountain. However, it is the sweeping panorama of brown peaks stretching from Slieve Binnian to Slieve Donard that impresses the most – a vista that also includes a backdrop of Slieve Bearnagh's jagged tors and Slieve Meelbeg's rounded hump. In clear conditions, even the Isle of Man can be seen across the Irish Sea.

From the summit, head north-west along the crest to reach an area graced by large rounded boulders and massive granite outcrops. From there, descend north-west on predominantly grassy terrain toward a ladder stile at the Mourne Wall. You are ultimately aiming for the col known as the Bog of Donard under the southern slopes of Slieve Donard.

As you reach the wall, the extent of ground erosion increases, making underfoot conditions boggy and squelchy when wet – hence the name Bog of Donard! Some walkers even choose to clamber up the wall and walk across its top just to escape the bog. Whichever way you choose, continue until reaching a stile at the col.

Do not cross the stile but instead go right and descend eastward on a stony and rocky track to reach an old quarry at Crannoge. A switchback path leads downhill to pass the quarry on the right and its mini-amphitheatre of vertiginous cut rocks. It then veers left onto a broad gravel track, passing a cutting shed where old granite blocks cut and split by quarry workers still remain.

Crannoge quarry.

The wedge marks around the edges are evidence of the 'plug-and-feathers' method of cutting stone. A small iron wedge (plug) is inserted between two thin pieces of hard steel (feathers) in a circular hole cut into the stone. The line for cutting includes an entire row of plugs which are struck with a hammer to split the stone.

Large sections of the old quarry track are lined with granite slabs. Continue along the track to pass under an unused railway line running along the hillside at Carr's Face above to the right. Large granite slabs were once hewn from this area for use as ornamental stone or as foundation blocks in construction works.

The track gradually descends for around 1.7km to meet the ladder stile at Point A once again. Cross the stile and retrace your steps back to the start.

Looking south-west from the summit of Chimney Rock Mountain toward Slieve Binnian.

Slievenaglogh (N) to Slieve Commedagh via Hare's Gap

The Mournes' most dramatic mountain pass, an enjoyable ridge across three peaks, fascinating rock formations and an old smugglers' path – what more can you ask for?

Grade:	3
Distance:	12.5km (7¾ miles)
Ascent:	640m (2,100ft)
Time:	4¼–5¼ hours
Map:	OSNI 1:25,000 *The Mournes Activity Map* or OSNI 1:50,000 Sheet 29

Start/Finish: Car park at Meelmore Lodge (grid ref: **J 306**₁₁ **307**₉₅).

Getting there: From Kilkeel: Take the Moyad Road (B27) out of Kilkeel. After around 13km (8 miles), the B27 goes left at a junction toward the Spelga Dam. Leave the B27 here and continue ahead on Slievenaman Road. Reach a fork after passing some forestry and Fofanny Dam on the right. Take the right fork and continue for around 400m to reach a crossroads. Turn right here into Trassey Road. The narrow road soon crosses a river before veering left around a bend. It then straightens to pass some houses and a red-roofed bungalow before reaching Meelmore Lodge on your right. **From Newcastle:** Follow directions from Newcastle to Bryansford along the Bryansford Road (B180). Pass the Barbican Gate entrance of Tollymore Forest before reaching a T-junction. Turn left here along the B180 towards Hilltown, passing the gates of Tollymore Forest and its Mountain Centre on the left. The Trassey Valley opens up on the left once the forestry ends. Soon, ignore Tullyree Road to your right and reach a bend and a big white house around 250m further on. Opposite the house is Trassey Road, which is signposted, as is Meelmore Lodge. Turn onto Trassey Road and go over Clonachullion Bridge. Follow the narrow road uphill past Trassey car park. The road veers right, then straightens and, after another 700m, reaches Meelmore Lodge on the left.

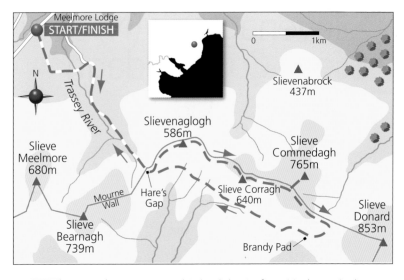

The next three routes in this book begin from Meelmore Lodge (www.meelmorelodge.co.uk). The Lodge offers self-catering accommodation, camping facilities, a bistro and café. At the time of writing, the car park was free during the day and cost £4 to park overnight.

The initial part of this route meanders along the Trassey Track to Hare's Gap, by far the most dramatic mountain pass in the Mournes. Its sharp outline is the legacy of retreating ice over its north-west/south-east alignment. The highlight of the route is an exhilarating ridge walk from Slievenaglogh (N) culminating at Slieve Commedagh, the second highest mountain in the Mournes.

The return journey passes under the curious outcrops of The Castle along an old smugglers' route known as the Brandy Pad. Back in the eighteenth century, when smuggling was commonplace, you might have heard ponies' hooves at night in these parts. The ponies were laden with illicit stock, mainly brandy but also tea, coffee, tobacco, soap, wine and silk. These contraband goods were shipped from the Isle of Man to the rugged coast south of Newcastle, funnelled up the Bloody Bridge River, along the Brandy Pad, then to Hare's Gap, exiting the mountains by way of Trassey and finally to Hilltown for distribution.

Route Description

Walk out of the car park with Meelmore Lodge to your left. Then turn left onto a tarmac lane leading south-east toward the mountains. The lane passes the open camping grounds of the lodge on the left and is soon flanked by stone walls. After a gradual rise, reach a ladder stile along a wall.

Meelmore Lodge.

Climb over the stile, then turn left onto a path indicated by Mourne Way/Ulster Way signposts. A well-trodden path runs beside the wall, soon becoming intermittent and boggy in places. After around 350m, the path meets the Trassey River and one of its tributaries – use stepping stones to cross both. Note that the rivers may be difficult to cross during or after heavy rainfall. Should this be the case, turn right and cross further upstream, before making your way back towards the wall.

Not long after, there is a gate on the left at a break in the wall. Here, the path meets the Trassey Track, which flanks a sheepfold to its right. The U-shaped Hare's Gap can now be clearly seen ahead in the distance. Now, simply follow the broad gravel track as it goes right again and heads south-east towards the gap.

Soon, the track passes under the mighty Spellack – a frowning, vertiginous granite face that looms away to the right. Its many buttresses and gullies owe their present form to the glacial ice that once swept across an older lining of rock around 10,000 years ago. Today, its sheer precipices are a haven for rock climbers on routes with intriguing names such as Ariel, Scarface, Cabin Cruise and Pegasus.

The track is rocky in places and forks after it crosses the Trassey River. Now, go left and then left again to ascend an indistinct, rocky path on a moderately steep slope littered with rocks and boulders until reaching Hare's Gap. Climb the ladder stile at the wall to meet a large cairn perched on a flat grassy area with scattered rock.

This is a good spot to appreciate the range of mountains that surrounds the wide valley ahead. The distinct outline of the Brandy Pad contouring

Looking towards Spellack from the Trassey River.

across the hillside can now be seen to the left. The immediate landscape is barren, apart from the Mourne Wall snaking up the mountains in either direction from Hare's Gap – to the right it rises south-west to Slieve Bearnagh, and to the left it runs north-east to Slievenaglogh (N).

Turn left now and with the wall to your left, ascend a flight of steep, granite steps. Ascend uphill a little further at the end of the steps and continue to reach a large cairn near some rock slabs on the summit of Slievenaglogh (N) (grid ref: **J 327**84 **291**06).

From Slievenaglogh (N), simply keep the Mourne Wall to your left and follow the broad ridge as it undulates before rising to reach a small cairn on the next summit, Slieve Corragh (grid ref: **J 337**10 **286**02). The view south is now quite splendid. At once you will notice the Ben Crom Reservoir, tucked under the pointed top of Ben Crom to its right. A host of other peaks can be appreciated, but the ones that draw most attention are the jagged tops of Slieve Binnian (distant left) and Slieve Bearnagh (nearer right).

When ready, descend south-east to the col below Slieve Corragh. This is followed by a ridge that leads to a steep slope rising towards Slieve Commedagh. This is actually one of the narrowest ridges in the area, but the head-height Mourne Wall obstructs the view on the left (northern) side, minimising the exposure.

It is a shame, as the Pot of Legawherry sits behind the wall, so it is worth standing on tiptoe to peer over, or to look back to try and catch a glimpse of the pot's rocky and barren recesses as height is gained. It is also worth looking back at the magnificent Mourne Wall snaking toward Slieve Corragh – a structure of truly monumental proportions.

Meet a pipe dispensing clear spring water on the ascent, a useful top-up for your water bottle if needed. Soon, as the slope relents, reach a watchtower with the date 1913 carved above the doorway lintel. There is a ladder stile here too at the southern shoulder of Slieve Commedagh (*Sliabh Coimhéideach*, 'mountain of watching').

Climb over the stile, then head north-east on the broad summit area following a vague path to reach the large cairn on the summit (grid ref: **J 346**$_{14}$ **286**$_{14}$), some 250m further on. The cairn sits on the foundations of a larger, older cairn – probably an ancient burial cairn. The summit provides exceptional views across the col to the south-east over to Slieve Donard.

The Mourne Wall extending towards Slieve Corragh, with Slieve Bearnagh in the distance.

Retrace your steps back to the Mourne Wall and watchtower from the summit cairn. Now, with the wall to your right, veer left and descend toward the col below. Views south along the Annalong Valley and its surrounding peaks are prominent over low sections of the wall. The steep profile of the Mourne Wall rising ahead to the summit of Slieve Donard is also impressive, and is best appreciated during the descent to the col.

Once at the col, use the ladder stile to surmount the wall before going right to descend and meet the Brandy Pad. Veer right (north-west) again now as the path meanders below some curiously shaped rocky pinnacles, buttresses and outcrops, known as The Castle. Steep gullies are riven into its steep slopes, where ravens roam and nest. The area above is also a haven for rock climbers on routes such as Born Again, Feeling the Crunch and Archibald.

Continue along the Brandy Pad for around 3km or so until reaching Hare's Gap once again. The distinct path of the Brandy Pad initially passes above the long, barren Annalong Valley to the left before gradually rising up some rocky slabs to reach a large pile of rocks. It later dips and then crosses a stream before undulating north-west, giving views of Ben Crom Reservoir away to the left and the pointed tors of Slieve Bearnagh in the distance.

Once at Hare's Gap, simply retrace your steps back to the car park at Meelmore Lodge.

Slieve Meelmore, Slieve Meelbeg and Slieve Loughshannagh

Take in three rounded Mourne summits, trek the Ott Track and visit Fofanny Dam – a bag of varied goodies!

Grade:	3
Distance:	12km (7½ miles)
Ascent:	735m (2,411ft)
Time:	4¼–5¼ hours
Map:	OSNI 1:25,000 *The Mournes Activity Map* or OSNI 1:50,000 Sheet 29

Start/Finish: Car park at Meelmore Lodge (**J 306**11 **307**95). If you have a second car, leave it at the car park along the road (grid ref: **J 292**85 **297**29) to reduce the length of the walk by around 1.5km (1 mile) or 20–30 minutes.
Getting there: As described in Route 4.

This is the second of three routes in the book starting and finishing at Meelmore Lodge. The aim is to walk over three dome-shaped tops, all linked by the Mourne Wall, to the south-west of the lodge.

Meelmore Lodge is named after the first top, whose height is erroneously listed in older maps as 704m instead of its actual height of 680m. Not far away is the second top, Slieve Meelbeg; it is similar in shape to Slieve Meelmore, but appears to be a little lower than the latter when viewed from the north. This optical illusion is probably the reason the Irish names of these mountains do not match their respective heights. Slieve Meelbeg (*Sliabh Maol Beag*) translates to 'Little Bald Mountain' and Slieve Meelmore (*Sliabh Maol Mór*) means 'Big Bald Mountain' – however, Meelbeg, at 708m, is actually higher than 680m Meelmore.

The third top, Slieve Loughshannagh, is named after the lake due south of it. It is the last in our trio of summits before dropping down to link up with the Ott Track, a popular access path for walkers in the western end of the High Mournes. A brief interlude on tarmac is followed by a jaunt along the Mourne Way/Ulster Way, passing the eastern end of Fofanny Reservoir before returning to Meelmore Lodge.

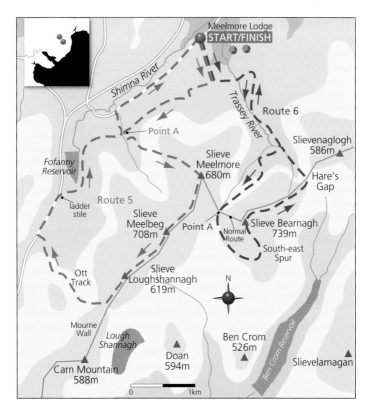

Approaching the stone tower at the corner of the Mourne Wall on Slieve Meelmore.

Stone tower, summit cairn and the Mourne Wall on Slieve Meelmore, as seen from Slieve Meelbeg.

Route Description

Walk out of the car park with Meelmore Lodge to your left. Then turn left onto a tarmac lane leading south-east toward the mountains. The lane passes the open camping grounds of the lodge on the left and is soon flanked by stone walls. After a gradual rise, reach a ladder stile along a wall.

Climb over the ladder stile, then turn right to follow an eroded path that runs alongside the wall. The path is waymarked by Mourne Way/Ulster Way signposts and undulates along the foothills below Slieve Meelmore. Follow the wall on your right, but keep away from it to avoid boggy patches.

Cross a stream after about 200m before the path becomes more distinct and grassy, resulting in drier underfoot conditions. Continue to a ladder stile at a fence by a deep stream-cut ravine (Point A).

Leave the Mourne Way/Ulster Way here and go left, following a wall uphill. After around 100m, meet a grassy ditch running perpendicular to the slope. Turn left here and follow the ditch for just over 100m to its end (grid ref: **J 295**95 **293**10).

An indistinct, grassy path veers left (south-east) here, well away from the wall. The path becomes clearer as height is gained. Ascend this path to reach a viewpoint on the shoulder of Slieve Meelmore, which is mainly grassy but dotted with rocks (grid ref: **J 302**50 **290**23). The expansive vista of the flat, green countryside to the north is best appreciated from here. Also apparent are the precipitous crags that line the north-west spur of Slieve Meelbeg across the barren valley.

Ascend south-east from the shoulder on a slope of grass, heather, moss and scattered rock to reach a stone tower at a corner of the Mourne Wall on Slieve Meelmore (grid ref: **J 306**₁₁ **287**₇₀). This tower is one of three that provided shelter for the stone workers as they laboured to complete the wall in harsh weather conditions. The existing tower was recently restored in 2014 and has a stepped pyramidal roof with a lintel over the door inscribed with the year of its completion, 1921.

Views from here extend both near and far, but the most dramatic is the Mourne Wall rising steeply up to the rocky summit of Slieve Bearnagh across Pollaphuca. For the best views, climb over the ladder stile that sits just to the right of the tower. Another view that is worth a mention is the impressive ridge extending from Slievenaglogh (N) to Slieve Commedagh.

When ready, descend a spur to the south-west toward a col below. Keep the Mourne Wall to your left and before long pass a rocky cairn before meeting another intersecting wall. Pass through a low gap in the wall and continue ahead to reach a broad shoulder. Soon, the slope drops steeply to a col below.

With the Mourne Wall still on your left, pass a ladder stile at the col, then ascend the moderately steep slope to reach the summit of Slieve Meelbeg (**J 300**₇₅ **279**₂₁), which is marked by a large pile of rocks. The views from here are even better than from Slieve Meelmore. The Mourne Wall can be seen snaking down the long crest of Slieve Meelmore, with Slieve Bearnagh and its granite tors clearly visible to the east. The waters of Lough Shannagh, Spelga Dam and all the hills of the Low Mournes unfold

Slieve Meelmore (left) and Slieve Bearnagh (right) from Slieve Meelbeg.

in a sweeping view from the south to the south-west, one that extends as far as Slieve Foye on the Cooley Peninsula.

Still following the wall, continue south-west from the summit of Slieve Meelbeg, dropping down to the next col below. Climb over the ladder stile at the col and, now with the Mourne Wall to your right, continue uphill to reach Slieve Loughshannagh, whose summit is marked by a pile of rocks (grid ref: **295**00 **272**03). The pointed, rocky top of Doan is especially prominent to the south-east, along with all the other aforementioned views.

Next, descend south-west to the col below Slieve Loughshannagh. Before long, the Silent Valley reservoir appears behind Lough Shannagh in the distance. At the col, climb over the ladder stile at the wall.

The Ott Track now comes into view and can be seen leading downhill, taking a few bends before meeting the road. Leave the col here and descend on this track. Negotiate a boggy patch before meeting the track proper (grid ref: **J 287**15 **269**00 in case of mist). The well-defined track – a mix of gravel, stones and rocks – contours under the slopes of Ott Mountain before descending to meet Slievenaman Road.

As you descend on the Ott Track, Fofanny Dam can be seen away to the right, which you will be visiting shortly. Follow the Ott Track to reach a metal gate by the roadside. Use a ladder stile here, then go right on the road toward a small forest ahead.

There is a ladder stile at a wall before the forest boundary. Leave the road here and use the stile on your right to gain access to a path on the opposite end of the wall, signposted by a Mourne Way/Ulster Way signpost.

An indistinct, grassy path runs alongside the edge of the trees. Follow this path to reach another ladder stile at a fence by the trees. Climb over the stile and follow a signposted path through the trees. The path has boggy sections and soon skirts around the corner of some trees before going right, away from the trees and onto a grassy track.

The path soon passes a footbridge on the right and soon reaches Fofanny Dam. Keep the reservoir on your left and continue to reach its northern end. Cross a metal footbridge with handrails here, followed by a small ladder stile at a fence. The waymarked path soon reaches a broad track slightly further on, where the stream-cut ravine at Point A earlier can be heard flowing ahead.

Leave the waymarked path here and veer left onto the broad track. The track runs alongside some trees to the left and soon reaches a metal gate with a ladder stile. Cross the stile to reach a car park with picnic tables.

Pick up your second car if parked here; otherwise, turn right and walk along Trassey Road for around 1.5km to return to Meelmore Lodge.

Slieve Bearnagh

A Mourne classic, this is a mountain that you will want to climb, and climb again.

Normal route		South-east route	
Grade:	4	Grade:	3
Distance:	8.5km (5¼ miles)	Distance:	9.5km (6 miles)
Ascent:	540m (1,772ft)	Ascent:	540m (1,772ft)
Time:	3–4 hours	Time:	3½–4½ hours

MAP: OSNI 1:25,000 *The Mournes Activity Map* or OSNI 1:50,000 Sheet 29

Start/Finish: Car park at Meelmore Lodge (**J 306**₁₁ **307**₉₅).
Getting there: As described in Route 4.

S lieve Bearnagh is a mountain of regal character. Its distinctive, rocky summit is crowned with a number of granite tors that makes you look up at once and take notice, whether nearby or from afar. Sculpted during the ice age around 10,000 years ago, these fascinating summit tors dominate the skyline when viewed from the Brandy Pad and from almost every peak in the High Mournes. The gigantic tors on Slieve Bearnagh are even more impressive close up. In an uncanny way, these commanding tors take centre stage for summiteers, oddly making the surrounding view less interesting than the tors themselves.

Another characteristic of Slieve Bearnagh is that its steep slopes are cut by deep hollows: to the north-west it plunges steeply down to Pollaphuca, and to the north-east a long crest descends to Hare's Gap. And so, it seems fitting then that the mountain derives its name from the Irish *Sliabh Bearnach* meaning 'mountain of the gap'. Even the brave builders of the mighty Mourne Wall were defeated by its unrelenting steepness. This is evident by breaks in the wall in areas where sheer, vertiginous rock slabs block the way.

The normal route up Slieve Bearnagh is to ascend the steep slope from the col at Pollaphuca. The path soon drifts away from the Mourne Wall

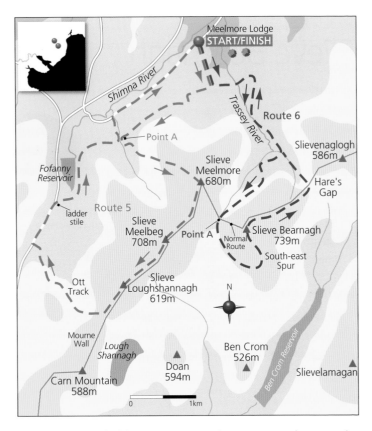

to avoid some rock slabs. However, maintain a course south-east on the boulder-strewn slope to reach a rocky outcrop on the summit plateau. Slieve Bearnagh's summit tor is located to the right of this.

Our route, however, is a slight variation from the norm – it isn't as steep and approaches Slieve Bearnagh via its south-east spur (effectively you will be ascending north-west toward the summit) from a broad, grassy shoulder. The surrounding views are good here and there is a glimpse of the valley on the eastern side of Slieve Bearnagh. This approach also means that you pass (or scramble!) all of Slieve Bearnagh's tors before meeting the Mourne Wall. It is also a quieter option – the normal route is usually busy, especially at weekends or public holidays.

Whichever route you choose, Slieve Bearnagh is a magnificent peak that deserves a return visit.

Hare's Gap from Meelmore Lodge.

Route Description

The start of this route from Meelmore Lodge to the Trassey River is described in Route 4. Cross the Trassey River (grid ref: **J 318**33 **291**91). Turn right onto a distinct track leading into a rock-strewn valley immediately after crossing the river. After a few bends, the track swings close to the river (now on the right) before veering uphill and away from it.

The track soon becomes rocky underfoot, with some granite slabs strung along some sections. Follow the track uphill to reach the col above.

Rocky tors on Slieve Bearnagh, with Slieve Donard rising in the background (right).

Slieve Bearnagh; its south-east spur can be seen rising towards some rocky tors on its summit.

The area here is known as Pollaphuca; the hard, fine-grained granite rocks here once attracted an influx of quarrymen and stonemasons in search of reliable stone. Before reaching the col, look above to the left at a wide, wrinkly crag known as the Bearnagh Slabs. These crags are popular with rock climbers, offering good friction routes around 80m/262ft high and with dramatic names such as Apocalypse Now, Greased Lightning and High Anxiety.

The col is tucked in a deep gap between Slieve Bearnagh and Slieve Meelmore. It is bordered by the Mourne Wall, which extends steeply uphill in both directions. Ignore following the wall in any case.

Climb over the ladder stile at the wall, then continue ahead. After around 100m, aim for a set of narrow, informal paths to the left. These paths contour across the rough hillside in a south-easterly direction.

Stay on the upper path and keep contouring – even if the path becomes vague – as it will improve again slightly further on. Soon, the tops of Ben Crom, Doan and even the distant Slieve Binnian come into view away to the right.

After around 1km (grid ref: **J 313**₅₇ **275**₁₉) from the col, go left and ascend a grassy and heathery slope to reach the spine of a broad spur. Here, rest if necessary and enjoy a panorama of peaks stretching from Slieve Binnian to Slieve Commedagh, with Slieve Donard peeking behind. The steep western face of Slievelamagan is particularly impressive.

When ready, veer left on the broad spur and ascend the slope towards Slieve Bearnagh. Although moderately steep, the terrain is mainly grassy so should pose no problems until reaching two rocky crags. Go around the larger of the two crags to its right, then face up a steep, grassy slope.

Ascend the steep incline to reach the base of two vertiginous rocky crags slightly higher. Here, a narrow path leads steeply up a rocky gully between the crags to deposit you on a flat, grassy area surrounded by massive, wrinkly tors (grid ref: **J 313**₃₆ **279**₁₁) – a great location!

With a growing sense of anticipation, go left around the tor in front on an undulating path at its base. Once the tor is bypassed, go right and after a slight rise, reach the summit plateau of Slieve Bearnagh. Its summit tor can now be seen away to the right. Take a detour towards it for a look, or optionally, you may choose to scramble carefully to the top using a notch at its northern end.

If not, continue north-west along the summit plateau toward the Mourne Wall to reach an outcrop of rock (grid ref: **J 312**₈₇ **280**₇₄). Now, with the Mourne Wall on your left, descend to a gap before rising again to reach Slieve Bearnagh's North Tor, where the wall stops.

This tor is also an optional scramble, as a path rounds it on the right before the long, steep descent towards Hare's Gap. The descent is initially on a grassy slope but this is soon strewn with boulders. After around 500m, arrive at a heathery shoulder dotted with rocky outcrops. Another steep drop looms ahead, before the wall is interrupted again at some rock slabs. Here, go slightly right to meet a flight of granite steps leading down to Hare's Gap.

Once at the safety of the gap, climb the ladder stile over the wall and descend the rocky slope beyond using intermittent paths to reach a track below. Cross the Trassey River once again and then retrace your steps from here back to Meelmore Lodge.

Slieve Binnian and Blue Lough from Carrick Little

Another magical Mourne peak full of tors and with outstanding views throughout. Why not plan a picnic at Blue Lough too?

Grade:	4
Distance:	10km (6¼ miles)
Ascent:	605m (1,985ft)
Time:	3½–4½ hours
Map:	OSNI 1:25,000 *The Mournes Activity Map* or OSNI 1:50,000 Sheet 29

Start/Finish: Secure car park (grid ref: **J 345**32 **223**10) around 350m from the main Carrick Little car park.

Getting there: From Kilkeel, drive along the main Kilkeel–Annalong road. After around 7km (4¼ miles), leave the main road and turn left onto Moneydarragh Road at Annalong. Reach a set of crossroads after around 1.4km (0.9 mile) and continue ahead along Oldtown Road. Reach a T-junction after another 2.4km (1½ miles). Turn left here and then immediately right into the main Carrick Little car park (grid ref: **J 345**07 **219**17). Pass the main car park on your left and continue for around 350m to reach the secure car park. The car park is to the left of the main track, below a house on an elevated site. At the time of writing it cost £3 to park for the day and £5 overnight.

The track at Carrick Little was once used as an old droving route for cattle, when it was common practice from late spring to the end of autumn for families to leave their homes and live in temporary huts or booleys in the hill pastures. Sheep rearing was secondary to cattle back then in the eighteenth century. The ownership of cattle was the symbol of wealth, and even land was payable in cows.

In AD 250, a Celtic chieftain, Boirche, was recognised as the 'cowherd to the High King of Ulster', a name that was bestowed on him based on the number of cattle he owned. Tradition suggests that Boirche once lived on the lofty summit of Slieve Binnian, and this led the Mourne Mountains to being known as *Beanna Boirche* or the 'peaks of Boirche' at the time.

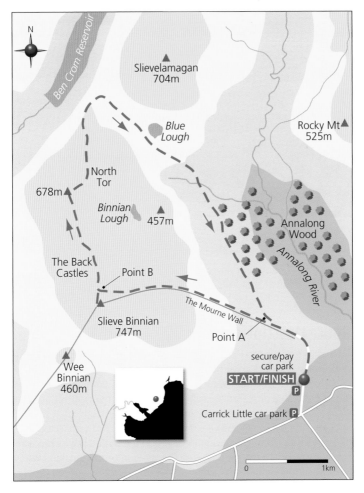

Like Slieve Bearnagh, the rugged crest of Slieve Binnian has a collection of fascinating granite tors of various shapes and sizes, some even resembling Easter Island 'Moai' statues. The bristly outline of these tors is easily identifiable even from afar and gives Slieve Binnian its distinctive character. The Summit Tor is monstrous and so is the North Tor further along the crest. There are also smaller tors in between such as the wrinkly arrangement of the Back Castles.

Normal walkers will be content to bypass these tors, but more experienced hillwalkers may choose to scramble up them. The approach route to Slieve Binnian's summit ridge via the Mourne Wall offers a great look into the barren Annalong Valley at the start. The route finishes with a

Looking towards the Annalong Valley, dominated by Slievelamagan, from the upper slopes of Slieve Binnian. Slieve Donard is the mountain rising to the right.

bang, with jaw-dropping views into the Ben Crom Reservoir near the end. There is also a fine spot for a picnic, or to simply bask in the sun, at Blue Lough before strolling back to the start alongside Annalong Wood.

Route Description

Turn left out of the secure car park onto a broad earthen track, flanked by stone walls. The track passes some buildings on the left, going gradually uphill to reach a set of gates around 550m further on. Enter the metal gate to the right, pass an information board, and follow the track for another 400m where it approaches the Mourne Wall (Point A).

Leave the track here and veer left onto a narrow, firm path to the right of the wall. Blocks of granite are installed on the path along sections to prevent erosion. To the right (north), the views into the Annalong Valley and its surrounding mountains improve as height is gained. In the opposite direction (south) and behind, the green Mourne plains and the blue sea unfold.

Follow the path beside the Mourne Wall uphill, ignoring any perpendicular, intersecting walls. It gets steeper with height and the path is rocky in sections. Near the summit and next to a ladder stile, the Mourne Wall ends abruptly when it runs into a sheer, vertiginous slab of granite.

Drift slightly to the right and away from the wall here. Follow a narrow, indistinct path steeply uphill toward a gap in a rocky cleft above to reach the summit area of Slieve Binnian (Point B). The small, flat area is guarded by steep, rocky crags on both sides; ahead, the Silent Valley seems a long way down. Here, a short detour is needed to reach the actual summit of Slieve Binnian.

With the crags looming (to your left) above, head left to follow a narrow path on the Silent Valley (western) side. After around 50m, the path intersects the wall at a low gap. Cross the wall and keep following the path as it loops back to the opposite (eastern) end of the ridge. A large tor now appears ahead, as the path goes left to reach the rocky summit of Slieve Binnian (grid ref: **J 320**65 **233**53) shortly. Some hands on rock may be needed to get to the actual summit.

Retrace steps back from the summit to Point B. The next section traverses the rocky crest of Slieve Binnian to the north. Before continuing ahead, you might want to heave yourself up a rock step to the left and stand atop a broad expanse of bare granite for the best views.

A sweeping view of the Mourne Mountains unfolds, from Slieve Muck in the west to Chimney Rock Mountain in the north-east. Closer at hand, the Silent Valley Reservoir can be seen, with Slievenaglogh (S) towering above. To the south, the green patchwork fields of the Mourne plains beckon, with the forested hill of Knockchree not far away. On clear days, Slieve Foye on the Cooley Peninsula can be seen. On very clear days, try and spot the Wicklow Mountains much farther south or the Isle of Man out in the Irish Sea.

When ready, head north/north-west along the ridge, passing several wrinkly tors, known as the Back Castles; each tor presents unique scrambling options if you choose. For walkers, a path bypasses the tors on the right with a gap in the wall roughly midway.

After the last tor is passed, the path dips down to the col. Look out for Binnian Lough on the right below as you descend. The path soon turns rocky in places before rising again. For purists, veer left and slightly north-west to summit Point 678m, but most walkers will be drawn in the opposite direction to the gigantic North Tor.

The section of the Mourne Wall where it runs into a rocky crag below the summit of Slieve Binnian. The route forwards goes between a gap in the rocky cleft to the right.

From the (western) Silent Valley side, the North Tor appears as two huge, wrinkly outcrops of rock separated by a steep, rocky and grassy cleft. A capstone, small in comparison to the tors, also lies above. If you wish to top this, then the easiest line runs from its back (eastern) end, on the Annalong side.

If you choose to continue walking, the path starts its steep, rocky descent north toward the col below. Around 250m before reaching the col is perhaps the most spectacular view in all of the Mournes. From the top of some rocky slabs here, Ben Crom Reservoir stretches before you, far, far below. Its craggy and scree-fringed slopes rise sharply from the water's edge, giving it a dramatic look. To the right of Ben Crom and in the distance are the unmistakable tors of Slieve

Ben Crom rising majestically across Ben Crom Reservoir, seen from rocky slabs near the col below Slieve Binnian and Slievelamagan. Slieve Bearnagh is the mountain to the right.

Bearnagh dominating the skyline, with the rounded humps of Slieve Meelmore and Slieve Meelbeg to its left.

Once ready, descend to the col. Blue Lough can now be seen away to the right (north-east) below the steep, rocky slopes of Slievelamagan. At the col, veer right along a distinct path and after around 700m, pass Blue Lough on the left. Head to the water's edge here, an idyllic area below the towering rocky crags of Slievelamagan.

Back on the path, continue to reach a T-junction. Admire the sheer crags to the right above. These fierce rock faces line the north-east end of Slieve Binnian, with names such as Blue Lough Buttress and Douglas Crag.

At the T-junction, turn right onto another path leading towards Annalong Wood, a sparsely populated forest which now appears ahead. It is common to hear a cuckoo's call in these woods from late April to late June. The male has a '*wuck-oo*' or an occasionally doubled '*wuck-uck-ooo*' call, whereas the female gives a bubbling '*pupupupu*'.

Soon, cross a river, using stepping stones to reach the edge of some trees on the left. A wall also runs up the hillside towards Slieve Binnian here. The path undulates along the edge of Annalong Wood and finally arrives at Point A once again.

From here, simply retrace steps back to the start.

Rocky Mountain and Annalong Valley

Another great Mourne viewpoint, this time from its eastern confines, followed by an unforgettable traverse along the spectacular Annalong Valley.	**Grade:**	3
	Distance:	15.5km (9½ miles)
	Ascent:	435m (1,427ft)
	Time:	5–6 hours
	Map:	OSNI 1:25,000 *The Mournes Activity Map* or OSNI 1:50,000 Sheet 29

Start/Finish: Secure car park (grid ref: **J 345**32 **223**10) around 350m from the main Carrick Little car park.

Getting there: As described in Route 7.

Rocky Mountain is an isolated and often neglected mountaintop on the eastern fringes of the High Mournes. It is hardly surprising that its higher and more accessible neighbours, Slieve Donard and Chimney Rock Mountain, are more popular amongst the hillwalking fraternity. Nevertheless, and despite being only 525m (1,722ft) in height, its summit is a unique vantage point, providing stunning vistas of the two highest peaks in the Mournes and also a sweeping view of the rugged mountain landscape across the Annalong Valley.

The Annalong is a long U-shaped valley stretching over several kilometres in the heart of the Mournes. A walk along its wide, barren recesses in such a dramatic glaciated landscape feels almost otherworldly. On a windless day, time seems to stand still. Towering buttresses, menacing gullies and imposing cliffs guard its western fringes; the natural landscape can be quite overwhelming, leaving one feeling humbled and insignificant in comparison.

This is a contemplative and fascinating route in a less-visited area of the Mournes. It is uncommon to meet other walkers, except for the short section midway along the Brandy Pad and near the end at Annalong Wood. For the most part, the heightened sense of isolation centred around the compelling Mourne landscape, prevails. Apart from the Challenge Walks, this is one of the longer routes in this book, so take your time and enjoy nature at its very best.

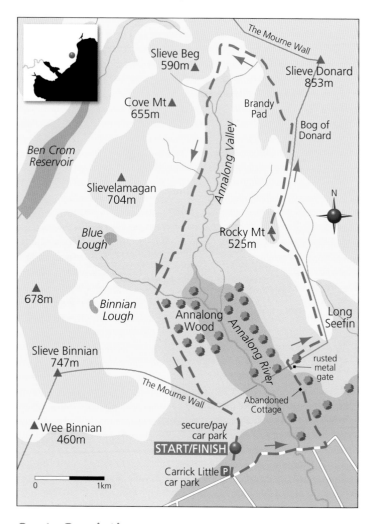

Route Desription

Exit the secure car park and head back towards the main road. Turn left there and follow the road as it dips down to Dunnywater Bridge. On a clear day, Rocky Mountain and Slieve Donard can be seen behind the trees away in the distance. In the opposite direction, a network of stone-walled fields borders the road to the right, with the Irish Sea as the backdrop.

The road rises after Dunnywater Bridge, soon passing Mill Road on the right. Before long, the stone-pillared gate of the Northern Ireland Water building is reached on the left. Leave the road around 20m after this and turn left into a lane (grid ref: **J 358**64 **223**28) with a stone marker bearing the numbers 256, 260a, 258, 264 and 266.

After passing the last house on the left, the lane gives way to a broad track that gradually rises alongside a forest. The track soon meanders past an abandoned cottage sitting within a granite-walled enclosure under a copse of trees on the right. After this, the track turns rocky before reaching a rusted metal gate (grid ref: **J 353**50 **233**50). If the gate is locked, climb over the stone wall to its left with utmost care.

Continue along the track, now flanked by stone walls and trees, from around 150m to reach another metal gate. Cross a ladder stile to the right of the gate and follow a path beside a wall along the edge of some conifers.

Looking westward across Annalong Wood to Slieve Binnian.

At the end of the trees, the path crosses a patch of gorse, before snaking alongside the wall, which extends up the hill. Follow the wall to its corner before going left up a slight rise to reach a ladder stile.

A sweeping panorama unfolds here across the Annalong Valley to the west. Slieve Binnian and its Summit and North Tors provide the picture-postcard view, with a backdrop of the rugged crown of Ben Crom farther away. The supporting cast includes the long crest of Slievelamagan and the precipitous faces of Lower Cove and Cove Mountain. To the north, Rocky Mountain beckons.

Ignore the ladder stile and continue ahead, keeping the Mourne Wall to your right. An informal path undulates on grass and heather beside the wall. Soon, the rounded profile of Rocky Mountain peeps ahead, flanked by the distinctive profiles of Doan and Slieve Donard.

Reach a ladder stile at the wall at the base of Rocky Mountain. Now, veer left away from the wall and ascend the grassy slope, which

Following the Mourne Wall with Rocky Mountain rising ahead.

is peppered with rocks. A vague path leads uphill, weaving between rocky outcrops to reach a broad summit area.

Soon arrive at a rocky cairn on the summit (grid ref: **J 350**₅₅ **252**₉₅) to be greeted by one of the finest mountain panoramas the Mournes have to offer. The best views are to the south-west, west and north. Across the Annalong Valley, Blue Lough presides at the foot of Slievelamagan, close to the Lamagan Slabs, a haunt of rock climbers. To the right, the precipitous crags of Lower Cove, Cove Mountain and Slieve Beg dominate and to the left Slieve Binnian sweeps across the landscape. The jagged alpine crown of Slieve Bearnagh peeks behind the col between Cove Mountain and Slievelamagan. To the north, the twin giants of Slieve Donard and Slieve Commedagh rise skyward. The Brandy Pad, our next port of call, can be seen cutting across the lower slopes of Slieve Commedagh.

Descend northward from the summit and head back towards the Mourne Wall. Follow the wall toward the Bog of Donard, a broad col below the southern slopes of Slieve Donard. Underfoot conditions before or at the Bog of Donard can be quite boggy and some walkers choose to clamber up on the Mourne Wall and walk along its top to avoid it.

Go left and away from the wall on reaching the ladder stile at the Bog of Donard. The path goes gradually uphill, soon turns rocky and forks around 550m further. Head left now onto the lower path, which is known as the Brandy Pad, an old smugglers' route in the eighteenth century. The path shortly meanders below an array of curiously shaped rocky pinnacles, buttresses and outcrops known as The Castle. Steep gullies split its steep slopes, where the *'pruck-pruck'* call of ravens can be heard. Along this section, the barren Annalong Valley can now be seen to the left, with its river twisting and turning for miles southward.

Some granite steps line the Brandy Pad, soon meeting a stream tumbling down from an arrangement of rocky pillars to the right above.

The view north to Slieve Commedagh (left) and Slieve Donard (right) from the summit of Rocky Mountain.

Immediately after crossing the stream, leave the Brandy Pad and veer left to descend along a path (grid ref: **J 343**66 **279**12).

The path eases progress on the otherwise heathery slope towards the Annalong Valley below. Keep your ears peeled for red grouse, with their distinctive *'go back, go back, go back'* call, in these upland heather moors. If disturbed, these medium-sized birds will suddenly shoot up from the heather and fly low with fast, whirring wingbeats.

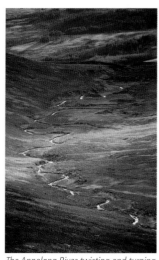

When the path divides, take the upper one, which runs above the valley floor, away from the river on the left. Before long, the path passes below the menacing gully of the Devil's Coachroad on the right, where you will feel compelled to look up at its steep, scree-filled and rocky recesses.

Next, the path crosses a stream flowing down from the col between Slieve Beg and Cove Mountain above. The path is now braided in places, soon passing under the towering buttress of Cove Mountain to the right. After crossing another stream tumbling down a gully from Cove

The Annalong River twisting and turning along the barren Annalong Valley, seen from the Brandy Pad.

Lough, it skirts close to the crags and boulder-strewn slopes of Lower Cove – another popular rock-climbing location in the Mournes.

Follow the path as it gradually drops down the valley for around a kilometre. The heather-covered slopes on either side are boggy, peaty and littered with boulders. The path soon broadens to a stony track before swinging right to meet another track.

Turn left at the track, cross a small stream, then after 500m cross a larger stream lined with granite slabs. Not long after, meet another path descending from Blue Lough to the right. Go left here, soon crossing another small stream before reaching the corner of Annalong Woods.

A wall runs up the hillside to the right here. Follow the path as it undulates along the edge of the sparsely populated forest for around a kilometre. Not long after, the path passes the Mourne Wall (which extends up the slope toward Slieve Binnian away to the right) and an information board before arriving at a metal gate.

Go through the gate and onto a broad track. The track is flanked by stone walls, passes some buildings on the right and gradually descends to meet the secure car park at the start.

The rocky pinnacles and tors known as The Castle, seen from the Brandy Pad.

Walks from the Silent Valley

The next four routes start and finish at the Silent Valley Mountain Park (grid ref: **J 306**19 **210**72). The park grounds are opened from 10 a.m. – 6.30 p.m. (April to September) and 10 a.m. – 4 p.m. (October to April). If you intend to stay beyond closing hours, mention it to the park attendant when you pay at the entrance.

Getting there: Head towards Kilkeel along the A2 from Rostrevor. Reach a T-junction with traffic lights at Kilkeel town. Turn left there in the direction of Annalong/Newcastle and continue for around 1km (0.6 mile) to reach a set of traffic lights just before a Eurospar shop. The Silent Valley is signposted here. Turn left, pass a Presbyterian church and continue along Carrigenagh Road for around 5.5km (3½ miles) to reach the entrance of the Silent Valley Forest Park. At the time of writing, a charge of £4.50 per car was payable at the entrance just beyond the main gates. Observe the one-way traffic system leading to the large car park at the southern end of the reservoir grounds.

    A café providing light meals and snacks is open 10 a.m. – 6.30 p.m. each day from June to August. From September to May (and including bank holidays) the café is open from 11 a.m. – 4 p.m. on Wednesdays and 11 a.m. – 6.30 p.m. Thursday to Saturday.

    Close to the café is a **visitor centre** with an audiovisual exhibition explaining the history of the Silent Valley and its reservoir.

    From June to August a **shuttle bus** service operates frequently between the Silent Valley car park and Ben Crom dam. This bus will reduce the length of the walk (one way) by around 4.8km (3 miles) and 1¼ to 1¾ hours for Routes 9 and 12.

    There are several colour-coded **walking trails** around the grounds, woodlands, reservoir, Kilkeel River and along the slopes of Slievenagore – ask for a leaflet for details when you pay at the entrance.

Slievelamagan, Cove Mountain, Slieve Beg and the Reservoir Trail

A delightfully scenic walk along the fringes of two large reservoirs and along a broad ridge, which culminates in a glimpse down into the fearsome gully of the Devil's Coachroad.

Grade:	4
Distance:	17.5km (11 miles)
Ascent:	775m (2,543ft)
Time:	6–7 hours
Map:	OSNI 1:25,000 *The Mournes Activity Map* or OSNI 1:50,000 Sheet 29

The view across the Silent Valley Reservoir with Slivenaglogh rising on the left.

Start/Finish: see page 63.

The Silent Valley is an impressive U-shaped glacial valley nestled between mighty granite peaks. A large reservoir fills most of its 5km (3-mile) length in its lower confines. Named after the valley itself, the

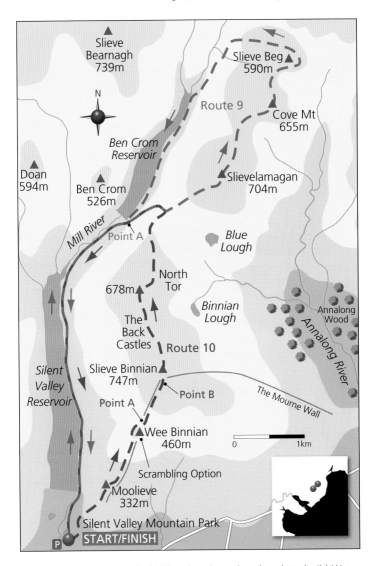

reservoir was completed in 1933 and took nearly a decade to build. Water flows into it from a second, higher reservoir, which is flanked by the steep slopes of Ben Crom and Slievelamagan. This 2km (1¼ mile) upper reservoir was opened 24 years later in 1957.

In the present day, both the Silent Valley and Ben Crom Reservoirs supply most of Belfast and County Down with up to 341 million litres (90 million gallons) of water daily. Before the reservoirs were constructed, the area was

On a rocky crag above the Devil's Coachroad on Slieve Beg, with Slieve Donard framed between the cliff edges.

popular with Cornish workers, who came to prospect for lead and silver in a quarry along the slopes of Slievenagore. These workers were known for their joyful singing and laughter, so much so the place was known as the 'Happy Valley'. However, the name was changed to the Silent Valley following the construction of the dam, because the prolonged blasting drove away the birds.

This route meanders along the eastern fringes of both the Silent Valley and Ben Crom Reservoirs during the early and latter stages of the walk. The walk in along the Silent Valley Reservoir to the high wall of the Ben Crom dam is on tarmac, whereas the section along the Ben Crom Reservoir is a narrow path.

In between the reservoir trails, the aim is to summit three peaks to the east of Ben Crom Reservoir. The first peak, Slievelamagan, is a towering mountain, with very steep slopes of scree and heather – so it isn't surprising that its name in Irish, *Sliabh Lámhagáin,* means 'crawling mountain', possibly referring to having to ascend the mountain with hands and feet in places due to its steepness.

A broad ridge extending north-east links Slievelamagan to two other summits over a series of dips and rises. The next summit, Cove Mountain, takes its name from a cave at Lower Cove; and the last one, Slieve Beg – quite easily the highlight of the day – features a mighty array of granite buttresses guarding the top of a steep gully known as the Devil's Coachroad.

Route Description

Take the footpath at the rear of the car park, passing an information board and toilets, to reach a small pond. The footpath soon meanders to the right of the pond, passing a playground and some picnic benches. Follow this footpath until it joins a tarmac road leading into the landscaped grounds of the Silent Valley Reservoir.

The road soon goes by the Education Centre, Tea Rooms and Visitor Centre on the right before reaching some large, old reservoir buildings.

A gap between the buildings leads to a spacious green area with embankment slopes further ahead. Take another footpath here which heads right to meet a flight of concrete steps.

Ascend the steps to reach the parapet of the Silent Valley Reservoir. Slievenaglogh (S) rises steeply to the left, Slieve Binnian to the right, and more shapely mountains are visible to the north across the far end of the reservoir.

Construction of the Silent Valley Reservoir was considered a great accomplishment of civil engineering at the time. One of the major difficulties faced by the workers was to find the actual base of the valley. Each time they thought they had reached the bottom only to discover it was just large boulders. When they eventually did, they had to build a cut-off trench made up of several cast-iron shafts and adjoining panels to form the robust frame of a 400m (¼-mile) long dam wall. The original ground level sits at the base of the 61m (200ft) deep reservoir, above the trench.

Do not cross the top of the dam but go through the main gates to the right of the reservoir. Now, with the reservoir to your left, follow a tarmac road for some 4.8km along the Silent Valley. Benches are installed along the road if you wish to sit and contemplate the beauty of the surroundings. At some stage along this scenic road, you will pass the spot where water emerges from the Slieve Binnian Tunnel. There is an information panel on the right of the road, so you won't miss it.

The Slieve Binnian Tunnel is 4km (2.5 miles) long and increases the water supply flowing into the Silent Valley Reservoir. The water is supplied through a pipe running under Slieve Binnian from the Annalong Valley to the east. Construction of the tunnel started in 1947 and was completed four years later by two teams digging from both sides of the mountain. The men dug the earth and rocks by hand, and blasted through solid granite in a confined space of around $6m^2$, using candles to help ascertain the straightness of their handiwork. When the two teams finally met in the middle they were astonishingly only around 50mm (2 inches) off!

Reach a turning circle shortly after passing the head of the Silent Valley Reservoir. The valley narrows beyond this and the road now runs near the Mill River on the left. Keep a lookout for feral goats along the valley floor and on the rugged hillside here. The birds have also come back to the valley since the construction stopped, so scan the skies for skylarks, ravens, wheatears and even peregrine falcons.

Soon the high wall of the Ben Crom Reservoir dam appears ahead, with the steep, scree-filled slopes and crags of Ben Crom rising above to the left. The road ends at a small roundabout at the base of the dam wall. Veer right here and ascend a flight of concrete steps to reach the parapet of the dam.

Do not walk across the dam, but cross a stile at the top of the steps (Point A). A footpath beyond the stile runs along the right of Ben Crom

Reservoir. Continue for a few metres on this footpath to meet another, narrower path on the right.

Leave the main footpath here and follow the subsidiary path diagonally uphill to reach a broad col between Slieve Binnian and Slievelamagan. The path rises quite steeply. It is mainly earthen but also rocky along sections, giving fine views down to Ben Crom Reservoir as height is gained.

Head left at the col along an indistinct path that weaves its way steeply up a slope of scattered rock and boulders to reach the summit cairn of Slievelamagan (grid ref: **J 328**97 **260**52). The surrounding view is good, especially across the waters of Ben Crom Reservoir to the jagged summit tors of Slieve Bearnagh away to the north-west.

Next, follow a path that drops north-east to a col below the next top. The path broadens and soon reaches a fork. Veer right at the fork and continue uphill to reach the rounded hump of Cove Mountain (grid ref: **J 336**66 **270**84), whose summit is marked by a pile of rocks on a granite slab. There are good views from here to Slieve Donard away to the east.

Descend steeply from the summit down to the next col. Cross a stream there before continuing uphill toward the next top, Slieve Beg. This top is unmarked (grid ref: **J 340**30 **275**95) but its highlight is a vertigo-inducing glimpse down the steep scree-filled gully of the Devil's Coachroad at the edge of some cliffs just before the summit. The top of the gully is flanked by vertiginous granite buttresses and crags, with Slieve Donard neatly framed in between.

The next section of the route is along a broad spur to the north-west away from Slieve Beg and toward the Kilkeel River. After around 800m along this spur, veer west, then south-west and descend steeply over rough ground to meet an indistinct path below. Turn left on the path and follow it to a stream. Cross the stream at a kink (grid ref: **J 329**60 **277**24) to meet an indistinct path on its opposite end.

The path contours along the steep hillside above a deep gorge to the right before dropping down to reach the northern edge of the Ben Crom Reservoir. This is an idyllic spot, framed by steep-sided mountains. The Kilkeel River flows into the reservoir here. On a dry and sunny day, you might want to cross the benign river to rest (or picnic) on a flat, green patch near the water's edge.

The remainder of the route is straightforward. Take the obvious, distinct path running to the left of the Ben Crom Reservoir. As you progress along this path, enjoy the ever-changing views across the reservoir toward the spectacular Ben Crom cliffs. It is all incredibly scenic, and the views behind you are just as good as the ones ahead.

After some 2km, the path meets up with the stile at the top of the steps at Ben Crom dam (Point A) once again. Descend the steps here and retrace your steps back to the car park at the start.

Moolieve, Wee Binnian and Slieve Binnian

Get your hands on rock in this challenging variation of one of the Mournes' best-loved peaks.	**Grade:**	4
	Distance:	11km (7 miles)
	Ascent:	715m (2,346ft)
	Time:	4–5 hours
	Map:	OSNI 1:25,000 *The Mournes Activity Map* or OSNI 1:50,000 Sheet 29

Start/Finish: see page 63.

There is always more than one way to climb a mountain, with some approaches more interesting than others. A different route gives fresh challenges, previously unseen vistas – and at times it can even feel like being on a different mountain.

Such is the case with Slieve Binnian. Back in Route 7, we approached this attractive peak from the south-east via Carrick Little, enjoying prolonged views into the Annalong Valley as we climbed. In this route, we tackle this mighty mountain from the south-west, following an interesting line over the lower, rocky summits of Moolieve and Wee Binnian. Besides an exceptional vista down to the Silent Valley Reservoir, this choice of ascent also provides contrasting views of mountains, plains and the sea.

Wee Binnian and Slieve Binnian rising in the distance from Moolieve.

Looking north along the broad ridge of Slieve Binnian from a rocky slab on its summit area. Lough Shannagh is the body of water on the left.

Although the summit of Moolieve is straightforward, the actual top of Wee Binnian involves some optional scrambling to reach its summit tor. There is a way to bypass this if you wish, but the final, steep line of ascent up Slieve Binnian is unavoidable.

The line follows the Mourne Wall rather steeply to reach the summit crest of Binnian. It is a good idea to get to grips with this tricky part of the route before attempting the Mourne Wall Challenge (Route 14), which traverses this section in reverse.

The rugged crest of Slieve Binnian has a collection of fascinating granite tors of various shapes and sizes. The bristly outline of these tors is easily identifiable even from afar, giving Slieve Binnian its distinctive character. The Summit Tor is monstrous and so is the North Tor further along its crest. There are also smaller tors in between, such as the wrinkly arrangement of the Back Castles. Normal walkers will be content to bypass these tors, but more experienced hillwalkers may choose to scramble up them.

Route Description

A footpath at the rear of the car park passes an information board and toilets to reach a small pond. Veer right at the pond and continue a few metres to reach a tarmac road. Cross the road onto a path across it, just to the right of the 'Way Out' sign.

The path splits into two almost immediately. Continue ahead to follow the distinct and narrow path gradually uphill through the trees. The path soon meanders under some electric lines before reaching a wall higher upslope.

Turn left and continue along a path that is flanked by a forested area on the left and a wall on the right. The path is lined with gorse and holly, and after around 200m, reach a ladder stile at the wall.

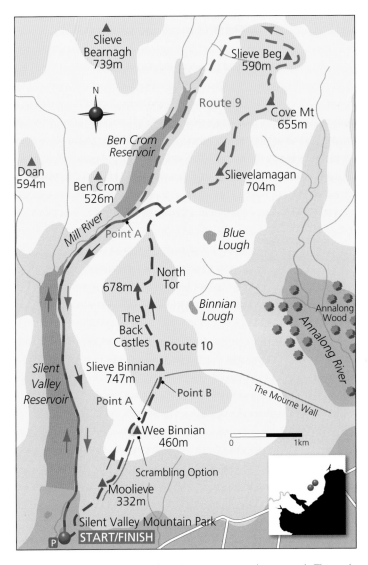

Turn right and climb over the stile to meet an indistinct path. The path snakes uphill on a moderately steep slope, close to the Mourne Wall to its left. Holly trees and gorse bushes are scattered all over the hillside. Meet a ladder stile where the Mourne Wall intersects another subsidiary wall higher upslope.

Standing atop a rocky tor on the summit ridge of Slieve Binnian. Slieve Donard is the cloud-capped mountaintop in the distance.

Climb over the ladder stile, then turn right to follow the Mourne Wall (now on your right) uphill. The slope is steep initially but later relents to reach the broad, grassy and rocky summit of Moolieve (grid ref: **J 312**72 **218**37). The rocky bulge of Wee Binnian can be seen further ahead from here, with Slieve Binnian and its rocky tors protruding behind.

The contrast of the landscape on either side of the wall is quite profound. Away to the north-west, Slievenaglogh (S) rises steeply behind the Silent Valley Reservoir, and from there a string of Mourne peaks sweep northward to Slieve Bearnagh. Over the wall, the landscape consists of an immense patchwork of fertile, green fields bordered by granite stone walls. Farmhouses and modern homes also dot these coastal plains, which extend from the foothills to the sea.

From the summit, descend north-east where the Mourne Wall meets an intersecting wall. Cross the intersecting wall at a low gap and continue ahead to reach a saddle where a rusted iron gate fills a gap in the wall.

Ignore this gate and continue uphill towards Wee Binnian, still keeping the Mourne Wall to your right. After a boggy section, ascend a grassy slope until the wall ends abruptly at the steep, rocky crag of Wee Binnian.

If you do not wish to scramble up a line of rusted posts, go left before the end of the wall onto a narrow path which rounds the rocky crag on the Silent Valley (western) side in a semicircle. Once past the crag, the path veers right and back towards the Mourne Wall to meet a ladder stile at Point A. Cross the ladder stile here over the wall.

Optional ascent to Wee Binnian summit: Take the narrow path which flanks the rocky crag but stop halfway along the semicircle. Leave the path here and veer right to ascend a steep, subsidiary path toward the summit of Wee Binnian. Some rock steps and large boulders requiring easy scrambling pose the last obstacles before the rocky summit tor is reached (grid ref: **J 316**84 **225**71). From here, descend carefully to meet a path on the eastern side at a wall. Keep the wall to your left and follow it down to meet the ladder stile at Point A.

Keep the Mourne Wall to your left and follow the path uphill toward Slieve Binnian, which now looms imposingly above. The grassy path soon turns rocky as it weaves its way up the heather-clad slope. The slope steepens considerably with height and is strewn with large boulders; there might also be the odd easy scramble over some rock steps along the way.

Reach a large wedge-shaped boulder where the Mourne Wall ends abruptly at the base of a vertiginous rock slab. Go right here and away from the wall to outflank the rock slab along an indistinct path. The narrow path leads steeply up a rocky gully to reach the summit crest of Slieve Binnian.

The gradient finally relents here when you pass a large tor on the right and meet a rocky outcrop ahead (Point B, grid ref: **J 320**79 **231**76). Take the path to the right of the outcrop and follow it over a short distance to reach the rocky summit of Slieve Binnian (grid ref: **J 320**65 **233**53).

Retrace your steps to Point B and follow a path to the left of the outcrop to reach the wall once again. Climb over the wall to emerge on the Silent Valley (western) side, and continue to follow the path as it traverses under a rocky crag rising above you to the right. After a few metres, the path meets a large rocky slab. Go around it to the right then left to stand atop a broad expanse of granite rock.

A sweeping view of the Mourne Mountains unfolds from Slieve Muck to Chimney Rock Mountain. Closer at hand, the Silent Valley Reservoir can be seen, with Slievenaglogh towering above. To the south, the green patchwork fields of the Mourne plains beckon, with the forested hill of Knockchree not far away. On clear days, Slieve Foye on the Cooley Peninsula can be seen. On very clear days, try and spot the Wicklow Mountains much farther south or the Isle of Man out in the Irish Sea.

When ready, head north, then north-west, along the ridge, passing several wrinkly tors known as the Back Castles, each tor presenting unique scrambling options if you choose. For walkers, a path bypasses the tors on the right with a gap in the wall roughly midway.

After the last tor is passed, the path dips down to the col. Keep a look out for Binnian Lough on the right below as you descend. The path soon turns rocky in places before rising again. For purists, go left and slightly north-west to summit Point 678m, but most walkers will be drawn in the opposite direction to the gigantic North Tor.

From the (western) Silent Valley side, the North Tor appears as two huge, wrinkly outcrops of rock separated by a steep, rocky and grassy cleft. A capstone, small in comparison to the tors, also lies above. If you wish to top this, then the easiest line runs from its back (eastern) end, on the Annalong side.

If you choose to continue walking, the path starts its steep, rocky descent northward to the col below. Around 250m before the col is perhaps the most spectacular view in all of the Mournes. From the top of some rocky slabs here, Ben Crom Reservoir stretches before you far, far down below. Its craggy and scree-fringed slopes rise sharply from the water's edge, giving it a dramatic appearance. To the right of Ben Crom and in the distance are the unmistakable tors of Slieve Bearnagh dominating the skyline, with the rounded humps of Slieve Meelmore and, further left, Slieve Meelbeg.

Once ready, descend to the col, then veer left on a path that drops steeply to the south-west. The narrow path is rocky in places and cuts diagonally down the slope. Follow the path until meeting another footpath running alongside the reservoir below.

Turn left onto the footpath and, shortly after, reach the top of the dam of Ben Crom Reservoir. Do not walk across it, but cross a stile here to reach the top of some concrete steps. Descend the flight of steps to reach a small roundabout below, at the base of the high wall of the dam. Go left and follow a tarmac road that initially meanders near the Mill River before running alongside the Silent Valley Reservoir.

The road extends for some 4.8km to reach the main gate of the reservoir. Enter the gate to reach the top of the dam of the Silent Valley Reservoir. Descend some concrete steps here toward a large green area below.

Veer left at the green and walk between some granite buildings along a tarmac road. The road passes the Education Centre, Tea Rooms and Visitor Centre on the left. Follow this road to pass a playground and finally reach the pond again at the start.

Retrace steps from here back to the car park.

Slievenaglogh (S), Lough Shannagh, Carn Mountain and Slieve Muck

A challenging circuit over a rocky peak above the Silent Valley Reservoir, followed by a fine mountain crest on the western fringes of the High Mournes. A large, scenic mountain lake awaits in between.

Grade:	4
Distance:	15km (9¼ miles)
Ascent:	790m (2,592ft)
Time:	5¼–6¼ hours
Map:	OSNI 1:25,000 *The Mournes Activity Map* or OSNI 1:50,000 Sheet 29

The view north-east across the Silent Valley Reservoir towards Ben Crom Reservoir from the summit of Slievenaglogh. Doan (far left, in cloud) and the pointed top of Ben Crom are the hills to the left of Ben Crom Reservoir.

Start/Finish: see page 63.

Slievenaglogh (S) is one of the lowest peaks in the High Mournes. Despite the modest height of 445m (1,460ft), its steep, conical profile means it is one of the first tops that catches the eye at the Silent Valley Reservoir. Rising above the western flanks of the reservoir, Slievenaglogh (S) is an isolated and quiet peak in comparison to some of its higher and

Lough Shannagh from the eastern slopes of Carn Mountain.

more renowned neighbours in the area. Besides its excellent views to the north toward Ben Crom, it is also an essential top for those undertaking the Mourne Wall Challenge (Route 14). Its steep and rocky slopes make the ascent interesting, with the use of hands necessary in places. It is a good idea to climb it before undertaking the Mourne Wall Challenge.

The latter part of the route visits two summits linked by a fine mountain crest along the western fringes of the High Mournes. This section can be remarkably quiet, so there is a good chance you will have the mountains all to yourself. The views on both sides of the crest are superb, showcasing the peaks and landscape of both the High and Low Mournes.

Besides the three summits, the highlight of this circuit must surely be the large, natural lake of Lough Shannagh (*Loch Sionnach*, 'lake of the foxes'), resting at 400m (1,312ft) on a mountain plateau. This glacial lake fills a corrie at the foot of Carn Mountain and is surrounded by a ring of deeply gouged tops on three sides. Its deep blue waters are said to be enchanted – haunted by the ghost of Sheelagh, the fair maiden of the O'Haidth clan, also known as 'the maid of the mist'.

In days of yore, Sheelagh was pursuing a fox with her horse up into the misty High Mournes. The fox ran into Lough Shannagh, with Sheelagh and her horse giving chase. However, the fox suddenly disappeared in the thick mist. At this point, Sheelagh tried to find a way out of Lough Shannagh, but due to bad visibility ended up getting deeper into its waters until she and her horse drowned. Later, her lover Mahon, while hunting a doe in thick fog, arrived at the shores of the lake to hear the shrill cry of a woman's anguish. Mahon urged his steed into the lake. Deeper into its waters they went, until Mahon reached the spot where the cries were heard. But only a white doe was there, struggling to stay afloat. The enchanted waters rose all around Mahon and his steed, and they were never seen again.

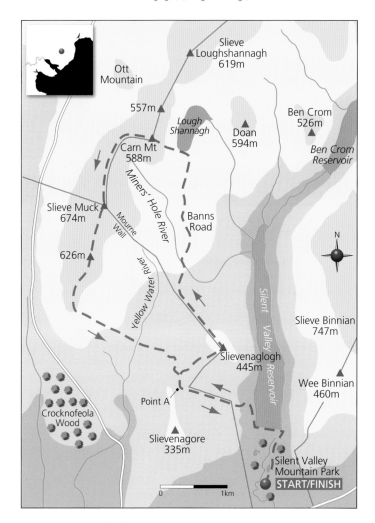

Route Description

The initial part of this walk from the Silent Valley car park to the top of the dam of the Silent Valley Reservoir is described in Route 9 (page 66). Once here, keep the reservoir to your right and walk across the broad tarmac strip on the parapet to its opposite end. Go right at a wooden information hut to follow a trail running alongside the reservoir.

The hulking mass of Slievenaglogh (S) now looms ahead, with Slieve Binnian rising majestically across the reservoir away to the right. Coloured arrows are displayed on a large rock where the trail forks. Go right to follow

The trig pillar on the summit of Slieve Muck, with the crenellated outline of Slieve Binnian and its rocky tors peeking behind the Mourne Wall in the distance.

the Black Trail on a firm, gravel path that rises gradually uphill to reach a wooden stile at a fence.

Cross the stile and continue along the path, which has been paved with rocky blocks to prevent erosion. After a switchback, the path meets another wooden stile (grid ref: **J 301**94 **220**93). Do not cross this stile, but instead veer right on an informal path.

The grassy path runs to the right of a fence initially, then later a wall. Veer away from the wall to avoid boggy sections, then later rejoin it. Climb over a ladder stile at the wall further uphill. Now, with the wall on your right, continue uphill to reach and cross an intersecting wall at a low gap. Keep following the wall on your right for around 250m to meet another ladder stile (Point A, grid ref: **J 292**91 **224**13).

Surmount this stile and follow a broad, grassy path for about 100m to reach a fork. Go right here onto a subsidiary path, then shortly right again onto another path that rises gradually uphill.

The path passes an old quarry and finally reaches a wall below Slievenaglogh's steep south-western flanks. Keep the wall to your right and ascend steeply uphill. The terrain is a mix of grass and heather at first but turns rocky as height is gained. There are some curious stone enclosures camouflaged amongst the rocky slabs and boulders along the steep slope. Stay close to the wall during the ascent, but if it gets too steep, move slightly away from it to find the line of least resistance. Nevertheless, some easy scrambling may be needed in places.

Pause to look back at the sweeping view of the sea, plains and hills as distant as Slieve Foye on the Cooley Peninsula. The steepness of the slope relents nearer the summit. Climb over a ladder stile at the wall, then head left to reach a small cairn which marks the top of Slievenaglogh (S) (grid ref: **J 298**80 **230**22).

Looking down on Banns Road and the Mourne Wall from Point 626m on the southern spur of Slieve Muck. Slieve Binnian and Wee Binnian can be seen rising in the distance. Slievena-glogh is the hill to the right (midground), to which the Mourne Wall extends.

The Silent Valley Reservoir sprawls along a deep gap to the north-east and east, with the mighty crest of Slieve Binnian sweeping across to the east. The pointed top of Ben Crom, visited in the next route, rises beyond Mill River at the far end of the Silent Valley Reservoir. Farther away, Ben Crom Reservoir, surrounded by a cirque of mountains, looks tiny from here.

When ready to leave, keep the Mourne Wall to your left and descend north-west from the summit on an informal path. After a steep midsection, the slope eases to meet a broad track at a rusted metal gate and ladder stile by the wall on the left. The track is known as Banns Road, once a drovers' route in these parts.

Ignore both the gate and stile and head right onto Banns Road which is mainly stony, but is rocky and earthen in places. The ground rises ever so slightly over a distance of around 2km and levels as it approaches Lough Shannagh. This is an enjoyable stretch after the earlier exertions on Slievenaglogh, boosted by the sweeping mountain panorama from Doan to Slieve Binnian away to the north-east and east.

On reaching Lough Shannagh, leave the track and veer left onto its sandy shores of fine, white granite gravel. This idyllic spot, dammed by a glacial moraine and surrounded by peaks, is ideal for a lunch stop.

Having rested, keep the water's edge on your right, and walk to the south-west tip of the lake. Follow an indistinct and intermittent path up a moderately steep slope there. The slope is a mix of grass and heather, heading roughly westward. Aim for a grassy strip to the left of a rocky patch, then continue uphill to Carn Mountain. The mountain panorama down to Lough Shannagh and across to Doan and Slieve Binnian from the summit slopes are exceptionally good. A pile of rocks marks the summit of Carn Mountain (grid ref: **J 287**95 **260**13) near a point where three walls intersect.

Climb over a ladder stile at the wall and enjoy views of the Spelga Dam and across to the Low Mournes away to the west. Now, with the wall on your left, head westward, following it down to a gap. The wall is punctuated by a rocky crag; bypass this to the right then veer back (left) to meet the wall again. Still keeping the wall to your left, head steadily uphill for around a kilometre to reach another ladder stile. Climb over the stile to meet a trig point on the broad, grassy summit of Slieve Muck (grid ref: **J 281**14 **249**96).

Next, leave the wall and descend on a broad, grassy spur to the south-west. This stretch of around 1.5km is exhilarating, providing expansive mountain views dominated by Slievenaglogh and Slieve Binnian across the barren stretch of the Yellow Water Valley away to the east. The spur narrows and begins to drop moderately steeply after passing a small cairn. A few hundred metres later, when a ribbon of road comes into view in the distance, there is a sudden, steep drop in the slope.

This is where you leave the spur (grid ref: **J 276**77 **234**62), but before you do, look roughly east-south-east across the Yellow Water River and pick out a green road heading uphill toward the slopes of Slievenaglogh (S). This is what you're ultimately aiming for so, when ready, veer left and descend steeply south-east on a grassy slope.

Take your time along this steep descent, but once the slope relents, traverse across a boggy section to reach Yellow Water River. Cross with care, especially on or after a wet day. The broad track of Banns Road lies above a small rise across the river. Depending on where you emerge on the track, locate the green road (grid ref: **J 289**04 **230**38) – if it helps it is near a distinct patch of tussocks.

Follow the green road south-east; before long, it dwindles into a path heading uphill to meet Point A once again. From here, simply retrace your steps back to the start.

Ben Crom and Doan

They don't quite reach Vandeleur-Lynam status, but these are two of the finest peaks in the High Mournes.	**Grade:**	4
	Distance:	17km (10½ miles)
	Ascent:	610m (2,001ft)
	Time:	5½–6½ hours
	Map:	OSNI 1:25,000 *The Mournes Activity Map* or OSNI 1:50,000 Sheet 29

The dam at Ben Crom Reservoir, with Ben Crom and its rocky crags towering above.

Start/Finish: see page 63.

Vandeleur-Lynam is a list of the 273 summits in Ireland, which are over 600m high with a prominence of 15m. While neither of the two summits featured in this route reaches the height to qualify as a Vandeleur-Lynam, they certainly do not disappoint. Both the lower summits of Ben Crom (526m/1,726ft) and Doan (594m/1,949ft) are rocky

At the cliff edge of Ben Crom summit, with its reservoir far below and Slieve Binnian rising behind.

gems amongst the High Mourne jewels. They are by no means 'soft summits' so must be treated with respect; the eastern cliffs of Ben Crom plummet to the reservoir below, while the narrow summit of Doan is safeguarded by a ring of small, rocky crags. The views from both summits are stupendous and perhaps the very best in all of the Mournes.

This route approaches Ben Crom via the tourist-popular tarmac road that runs alongside the Silent Valley Reservoir and Mill River. After summiting both tops, the route drops down to the shores of the idyllic Lough Shannagh, also visited in Route 11. Here, you may choose to link up with the previous route to include two further summits, Carn Mountain and Slieve Muck, returning by way described in that route. If not, simply meander down Banns Road before returning to base using the directions in this route.

Route Description

The initial part of this walk from the Silent Valley car park to the top of the dam of the Ben Crom Reservoir is described in Route 9 (page 66). Walk across the tarmac strip on top of the dam to its opposite end where a metal gate and ladder stile lie under the precipitous, scree-fringed cliffs of Ben Crom.

Cross the stile and go left onto a path which contours along the hillside. At a fork a few metres further, veer right onto a firm, narrow path. The path, which is rocky in places, ascends diagonally and steeply up the hillside. Take your time along this stretch while appreciating the lovely

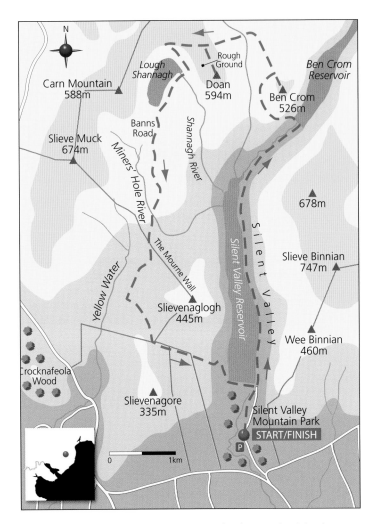

views toward the Silent Valley Reservoir in the distance. Look back too at the impressive headwall of the Ben Crom Reservoir, with Slievelamagan peeking behind it.

The path broadens and the gradient relents as you approach the top of the slope. Once the ground levels, the path goes right, skirting around the western slopes of Ben Crom. The conical peak of Doan soon emerges away to the left, with the view sweeping clockwise to the twin summits of Slieve Meelmore/Meelbeg and the jagged top of Slieve Bearnagh further north.

The path soon begins to head northward as it passes under the grassy slopes of Ben Crom. At any convenient point, leave the path and go right to ascend the slope. Aim for a strip of heather between some rocky pillars and a distinct patch of scree. The slope, covered with bilberries in the summer, steepens near the top.

The top of the slope is a broad spur from where there is a good view of the Ben Crom River, which twists and turns along a barren U-shaped valley below the eastern slopes of Doan. From here, a panorama of Mourne peaks sweeps clockwise across to Slieve Bearnagh culminating at Slieve Donard away to the north-east.

When ready to move, head right on the spur. A gradual ascent leads to Ben Crom (grid ref: **J 313**$_{05}$ **260**$_{25}$), whose summit consists of large, rocky slabs. Its eastern and southern ramparts are guarded by precipitous crags and cliffs overlooking Ben Crom Reservoir below. It is a dizzying view down. The gentler views are across the reservoir toward Slievelamagan, Blue Lough, Slieve Binnian and the Silent Valley Reservoir farther south.

Retrace steps from the airy summit to the broad spur and continue in a general north-westerly direction. A distinct path leads down the spur to reach an area of peat hags and blanket bog. Go left and pick your way between peat hags toward Ben Crom River. Here, at its upper reaches, it is just a stream. Cross it at any convenient point (for example at grid ref: **J 306**$_{03}$ **268**$_{17}$), then traverse a trackless area of rough moorland through more peat hags.

Aim for the top of a spur ahead, where a path appears. Lough Shannagh also comes into view here. Veer left onto the path that meanders south-eastward to the rocky summit of Doan. The path soon splits into two just before the summit. The left-hand option is more interesting and includes an easy, rocky scramble to reach the summit. The right branch is easier along a path, then up some rocky steps to gain the airy summit.

Either way, the rocky summit of Doan (grid ref: **J 302**$_{36}$ **262**$_{08}$) provides one of the finest 360-degree views in the High Mournes. All the Mourne giants can be identified from here: Slieve Binnian and its distinctive tors nearby, the broad slopes of Slieve Muck to the south-west, the Meelmore twins to the north, Slieve Bearnagh and its summit crown, and the line of summits leading to Slieve Donard away to the north-east. Cove Mountain rises in front of Slieve Donard, and another line runs south-west from Cove Mountain to the hulking mass of Slievelamagan. The rugged, rocky top of Ben Crom sits between Slievelamagan and Doan. The most scenic view is arguably south toward the Silent Valley Reservoir, where the entire Mourne landscape of mountain, hill, plains and sea may be savoured.

When ready to depart, retrace steps back along the broad spur, descending north-west for around 500m. Then leave the spur by heading left and down a rough slope for another 500m to reach a path below (grid ref: **J 295**$_{00}$ **266**$_{50}$). Turn left at the path and follow it south-east for approximately 500m. Then turn right and descend south-west down the slope, aiming for a stone shelter (grid ref: **J 296**84 **262**37) below.

Cross the outflow of Lough Shannagh to reach the stone shelter, then take the distinct path running across an area of decayed blanket bog and peat along the eastern end of the lake. The path broadens to a wide track, known as Banns Road, at the southern end of Lough Shannagh.

Follow Banns Road as it undulates down the hillside and soon crosses the Miners' Hole River. This river is named after a group of Cornish miners who once worked the area in the hope of extracting metallic ore from the local granite. The pebbly, stony and rocky track soon reaches a rusted metal gate and a ladder stile at the Mourne Wall.

The wall can be seen snaking up to Slievenaglogh (S) to the left. Ignore the wall and climb over the stile. Continue along the track for around 850m until it passes a green road on the left near a tussocky patch. Leave the track here (grid ref: **J 289**04 **230**38) by turning left onto the green road and follow it uphill where it soon dwindles into a grassy path.

At a fork, ignore a subsidiary path leading uphill on the left. Instead, continue ahead to meet a ladder stile at a wall. Climb over it then go left onto another path running to the right of the wall. Before long, the path crosses an intersecting wall at a low gap then after another 200m further it reaches another ladder stile on the left.

Climb over this stile, then turn right. The wall is now to your right as you descend on an intermittent path, which is boggy in places. Later, follow a fence downhill to reach a distinct path finally by a stile on the right (grid ref: **J 301**94 **220**93).

Ignore this stile and instead turn left onto the path. It descends down a bracken-filled slope and soon meets another stile after a bend. Cross this stile and continue until reaching a T-junction. Turn left there to soon reach an information hut with a wooden bench.

The top of the dam of the Silent Valley Reservoir can now be seen to the left. Walk along the tarmac strip to its opposite end, then go right to descend some concrete steps toward a large green area below.

Head left at the green and go between some granite buildings along a tarmac road. The road passes the Education Centre, Tea Rooms and Visitor Centre on the left. Follow this road back to the car park at the start.

Challenge Walks

Walking on the Mourne Wall.

The Mourne Seven Sevens

This is a challenge to climb all seven peaks in the Mournes over 700m. It is a bit of a misnomer, as there are actually only six peaks over 700m. However, all heights are taken from the 1990 edition of the Ordnance Survey (OS) map, where one mountain, Slieve Meelmore, is incorrectly listed as being over 700m. They couldn't call it the Mourne Six Sevens, could they?

The route begins and ends at Donard Park in Newcastle. In this book, the seven summits are climbed in the following order: Slieve Donard (853m/2,799ft), Slieve Commedagh (765m/2,510ft), Slievelamagan (704m/2,310ft), Slieve Binnian (747m/2,451ft), Slieve Meelbeg (708m/2,323ft), Slieve Meelmore (704m/2,310ft in OS 1990 edition, 680m/2,231ft in newer editions) and Slieve Bearnagh (739m/2,425ft).

To make it more of a grand circuit, Slieve Donard is summited by a lesser-used line along its north-eastern spur via the Granite Trail. Alternatively, you could also take the more popular route up Donard by following the Glen River path via Donard Forest. This later involves an out-and-back to the summit from the col below. The only other part of the route that involves an out-and-back is the section from the col between Slieve Binnian and Slievelamagan, during the ascent of Slieve Binnian.

The Mourne Wall Challenge

This is a true Irish mountain classic. The core of this epic walk involves following the course of a 35km (22-mile) long stone wall known as the Mourne Wall or Black Ditch. For 27 years from 1957, this challenge was a yearly affair organised by the Youth Hostels Association of Northern Ireland, growing to be the largest mass participation event held in the Irish mountains, with some 4,000 challengers on a single day. However, this contributed to a severe amount of erosion to the hillside, and amid growing concerns the organised event was discontinued.

The Mourne Wall Challenge covers the following fifteen summits: Slieve Binnian (747m/2,451ft), Wee Binnian (460m/1,509ft), Moolieve (332m/1,089ft), Slievenaglogh (S) (445m/1,460ft), Slieve Muck (674m/2,211ft), Carn Mountain (588m/1,929ft), Slieve Loughshannagh (619m/2,031ft), Slieve Meelbeg (708m/2,323ft), Slieve Meelmore (680m/2,231ft), Slieve Bearnagh (739m/2,425ft), Slievenaglogh (N) (586m/1,923ft), Slieve Corragh (640m/2,100ft), Slieve Commedagh (765m/2,510ft), Slieve Donard (853m/2,799ft) and Rocky Mountain (525m/1,722ft).

Built out of local granite, the Mourne Wall links the summits of these fifteen mountains. The top of the wall is high enough (2.4m/8ft) to require one to stand on tiptoe for a view across to its other side, and wide enough (0.9m/3ft) to walk on. Planning for this monumental structure began in 1893, when the Belfast City and District Water Commissioners purchased land from Lord Kilmorey and the Annesley family. The water commissioners identified the High Mournes as an ideal natural source for supplying up to 30 million gallons of clean water per day to an ever-expanding Belfast.

A plan was devised to build a wall to surround the 9,000 acre (3,642 hectare) mountain catchment area of the High Mournes. Completed in 1922, it took 'hard men with herculean strength, powerful shoulders and hands like shovels' almost 18 years to build. These were men who worked weekdays on the mountain, sleeping by the cold stone at night, only returning to their families late on a Friday night. In biting winter winds and lashing rain, hundreds of thousands of tons of granite boulders were prised and shaped from the bedrock of the Mournes and painstakingly put in place by the men without the use of mortar. Ironically, the only mortar used was in the stone towers that provided shelter to the workmen on the summits of Slieve Meelmore, Slieve Commedagh and Slieve Donard.

Optional Transport

Due to the nature and length of both challenge walks, it is useful to have a Plan B, in case you need to retire from either route without finishing. Here are two transport options to keep in mind: **Mourne Rambler** bus service operated by Ulsterbus during the summer months. The bus circles the Mournes and the timetable is available at: www.translink.co.uk

Mourne Shuttle Service – a 16-seat minibus provides a hillwalker service, including a bespoke pick-up/set-down in all regions of the Mournes. It includes stops at key walking start and finish points described in this book, such as Meelmore Lodge, Donard Park, Bloody Bridge and Carrick Little: tel: +44 (0)7516 412 076.

The Mourne Seven Sevens

Challenge yourself to climb all seven peaks in the Mournes over 700m (well, one under 700m if you go by newer maps)!

Grade:	5
Distance:	33km (20½ miles)
Ascent:	2,660m (8,727ft)
Time:	13–15 hours
Map:	OSNI 1:25,000 *The Mournes Activity Map* or OSNI 1:50,000 Sheet 29

Start/Finish: Donard Park main car park (grid ref: **374**₄₂ **305**₇₀).

Getting there: If approaching from Kilkeel/Annalong/Bloody Bridge (A2) along the Kilkeel Road, follow signs for Donard car park before reaching Newcastle. If approaching from Bryansford (B180)/Dundrum (A2), head into Newcastle and aim for the coast road to Bloody Bridge/Annalong/ Kilkeel (A2). Follow signs for Donard car park before reaching the coast road.

Escape routes: Due to the length of this walk, it is imperative to bail out if necessary. There are two points along the route where this is possible: (1) Ben Crom Dam: follow a tarmac lane south-west, then later south along the Silent Valley Reservoir to reach the Silent Valley car park; (2) Hare's Gap: descend north-west to reach the Trassey Track and follow it back to Meelmore Lodge.

Route Description

Take a gravel track at the back (southern end) of the main car park. The track is bordered by a green fence and meanders alongside Donard Park to reach Donard Wood. Enter the woodlands and ascend its leafy slopes. With the Glen River running not far to the left, continue uphill to reach Donard Bridge (Point A).

Turn left and cross the bridge, where a waterfall tumbles down rock shelves to the right. Head right immediately after the bridge onto a cobbled path that runs beside the river, which is now to your right.

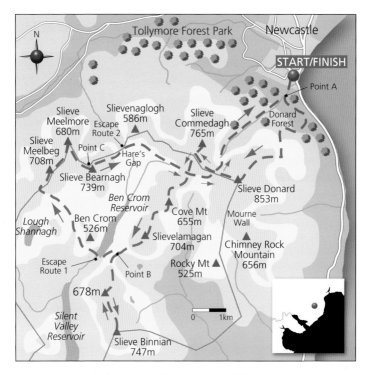

Leave the cobbled path and veer left at a fork onto a surfaced forest track. After a metal barrier, the track leads uphill through the woods and later passes an arched granite enclosure with '1842' inscribed on a stone plaque atop.

Ignore all subsidiary tracks on the right after this and stay on the main track as it contours along the forested slopes. Finally, reach a 'Granite Trail' information board at the base of a flight of steps leading steeply uphill to the right.

Turn right and ascend the steps, pausing only to look back at Dundrum Bay, which is visible through the trees as height is gained. Continue uphill to reach a Shoddy Hut, ladder stile and wooden gate at a fence.

Climb over the stile then veer right onto a path that runs near the forest edge. The imposing mass of Millstone Mountain rises to the left as you follow the path gently uphill to meet another wooden gate and ladder stile.

Enter the gate, then go left to reach the base of a large quarry. Take a path to the right of a large zinc hut with a concrete base. Follow a fence on the left and descend to reach a rusted metal gate by a wall.

Slieve Donard (right) and Slieve Commedagh (left), the first two summits of the Mourne Seven Sevens.

Head left immediately toward a small concrete hut to reach an informal, earthen path. Follow this path uphill to reach a flat area above the quarry, giving fine views, from Castlewellan to Dundrum Bay away to the north and east.

The path turns grassy and later runs to the right of a stream-filled gorge. Continue uphill to reach a flat, boggy area. Go right here and head westward to reach a grassy shoulder below the spur that rises toward Slieve Donard.

Ascend the spur, whose gradient gets steeper with height; the terrain becomes increasingly rocky. Reach the Lesser Carn and a stone shelter after negotiating a small boulder field. The steepness finally relents when you reach the Great Carn and trig pillar on the top of a granite tower, marking the summit of Slieve Donard (grid ref: **J 357**98 **276**89), the highest point in Northern Ireland.

From the summit, keep the Mourne Wall to your left and veer right to descend steeply toward the col below. Next, follow the wall uphill until reaching a ladder stile by a watchtower. Veer right there and head north-east to reach the large cairn on the summit of Slieve Commedagh (grid ref: **J 346**14 **286**14) some 250m further on.

Retrace steps back to the ladder stile and watchtower. Climb over the stile, then leave the comfort of the Mourne Wall to descend a steep slope in a general south-south-west direction. Aim for the well-defined Brandy Pad track below just to the left of a broad col.

Ignore the Brandy Pad and continue south-west on a gradual rise toward the unmarked summit of Slieve Beg (grid ref: **J 340**30 **275**95). Peer down the Devil's Coachroad gully from just below the summit before continuing along the broad ridge toward Slievelamagan. Drop west-south-west to the col below, then up south-south-east to gain the summit of Cove Mountain (grid ref: **J 328**82 **261**30), marked by a pile of rocks on a granite slab. Descend to the next col, before a more sustained rise up a moderately steep slope to reach the summit cairn of Slievelamagan (grid ref: **J 321**₆₂ **357**₇₁).

Descend steeply to the south-west from the cairn, zigzagging down an indistinct path on a slope of boulders and scattered rock to reach a col (Point B) below. From here continue southward up the next slope, later veering right to reach Slieve Binnian North Tor. Descend to a broad gap from here before climbing south-east over the wrinkly tors of the Back Castles (for walkers, a path bypasses the tors on the left) before the final pull to a large rock slab on the summit area of Slieve Binnian.

Some might choose to scramble up the actual top of

Looking eastward to Slieve Donard from the rocky clifftop of Slieve Beg.

Slieve Binnian, its rocky Summit Tor. However, there is an easier way to gain the top. Flank the Summit Tor on the right (Silent Valley or western side) and follow a path at its base to reach a wall. Cross a low gap in the wall and continue to meet another large tor. Veer left and northward, back along the ridge, and then up some rock steps to reach the top of Slieve Binnian.

From the summit, retrace your steps back to the col at Point B. With Ben Crom Reservoir below, head north-west for around 100m, then veer left (south-west) to follow a narrow path that descends steeply and diagonally downhill to reach the top of Ben Crom dam.

Walk across the broad concrete strip on top of the dam to meet a metal gate and ladder stile. With the cliffs of Ben Crom looming above, cross the stile, then go left immediately onto a path that runs along the hillside. Leave the path after a few metres and go right at a fork. Ascend steeply uphill on a narrow but firm path, which is rocky in places.

There are fine views back toward the Silent Valley Reservoir, under the shadow of Slievenaglogh (S). Views back toward the headwall of Ben Crom Reservoir, with Slievelamagan peeking behind it, are equally good.

The path cuts diagonally along the slope, steeply at first before relenting on flatter ground at the top (grid ref: **J 310**₂₉ **255**₀₀), somewhere

Looking down on Ben Crom Reservoir from just above the col at Point B. The route crosses the dam on top of the reservoir, and then goes up the hillside to the left of Ben Crom, before following the course of the Ben Crom River that runs between Ben Crom and Doan (far left).

below the southern spur of Ben Crom. From there, advance westward for around 200m to reach the eastern bank of the Bencrom River.

Now, follow the course of the river, northward initially then north-westward, to reach a slope rising to meet a ladder stile along the Mourne Wall. Note the terrain near the river can be boggy and rough so perseverance is needed along this section!

Arrive at drier conditions at the wall. Climb over the stile, go right and ascend the moderately steep slope to reach the summit of Slieve Meelbeg (grid ref: **J 300**$_{75}$ **279**$_{21}$), marked by a large pile of rocks.

Descend the next slope down to the col below, then up again toward the next summit of Slieve Meelmore. Pass a rocky cairn, then reach a ladder stile before a stone tower at a corner of the Mourne Wall (grid ref: **J 306**$_{11}$ **287**$_{70}$) on Slieve Meelmore.

Climb over the stile, then follow a wall on your left steeply down to a col at Pollaphuca below. The col sits below the rocky summit of Slieve Bearnagh, and to get there you must ascend steeply up a rocky slope. The path soon drifts away from the Mourne Wall, avoiding some rock slabs. However, maintain a course south-east on the boulder-strewn slope to reach a rocky outcrop by the wall (grid ref: **J 312**87 **280**74, Point C) on the summit plateau.

But the outcrop is not the actual summit. For this, you must go right and scramble up the rocky summit tor of Slieve Bearnagh, around 100m away. The easiest line is through a notch at its northern end.

From the summit tor, retrace steps back to Point C. Keep the wall to your left and descend to a gap before rising again to reach Slieve Bearnagh North Tor. Scramble up it if you must, but a path flanks it on the right before descending steeply down to Hare's Gap. Some granite steps are installed in steep sections just before the gap to prevent further erosion. A large cairn is perched on a flat grassy area of scattered rock to the right of the gap.

This is where all difficulties end. Veer right to join the Brandy Pad, a distinct path which contours along the slopes below Slievenaglogh (N), Slieve Corragh and Slieve Commedagh. There are fine views of Ben Crom Reservoir in the distant south before the path gradually rises to reach a large pile of rocks on a broad col. It later passes above the barren Annalong Valley to the right and soon enough under the peculiar rocky arrangement of The Castle to its left.

Leave the Brandy Pad soon after passing The Castle, veering north-east and up to a saddle above. Climb over the ladder stile and head towards a large cairn. Descend north-east following some steep granite steps, then later a path toward the Glen River below.

Cross the Glen River using stepping stones, then veer right onto a path made up of granite slabs. The path descends gently and is flanked by the imposing crags of Eagle Rock and the scree-fringed slopes of Slieve Commedagh.

Follow the path to reach the upper reaches of Donard Wood. The path runs alongside the edge of some trees above a boulder-strewn riverbed to the right. Look out for an icehouse on the opposite bank of the river just before reaching a bridge.

Ignore the broad U-shaped forest track but continue ahead on a narrow path through the woods. The path descends quite steeply over rock slabs in places and finally reaches another bridge further below. Continue to descend through the woods, with the river still away on your right. Later, as the slope relents you will reach Donard Bridge (Point A) once again.

Retrace steps from here back to the start.

The Mourne Wall Challenge

Northern Ireland's ultimate high-peaks challenge along the mighty Mourne Wall.

From Carrick Little or Silent Valley		From Meelmore Lodge	
Grade:	5	**Grade:**	5
Distance:	33.5km (21 miles)	**Distance:**	40.5km (25 miles)
Ascent:	2,860m (9,383ft)	**Ascent:**	3,080m (10,105ft)
Time:	14–16 hours	**Time:**	15–17 hours

Map: OSNI 1:25,000 *The Mournes Activity Map* or OSNI 1:50,000 Sheet 29

Start/Finish: Secure car park around 350m away from the main Carrick Little car park at **J 345**32 **223**10. At the time of writing it cost £3 to park here for the day and £5 overnight. Note that Carrick Little car park is also on the Mourne Rambler (summer only) and Mourne Shuttle Service bus routes.
Getting there: As described in Route 7.

Alternative secure parking:
Car park at Meelmore Lodge (grid ref: **J 306**11 **307**95), or from the Silent Valley car park at (grid ref: **J 306**19 **210**72). For directions to get here, see description in Route 4 for Meelmore Lodge and on page 63 for the Silent Valley. If starting from Meelmore Lodge, walk up to Hare's Gap (see description in Route 4), then pick up the Mourne Wall towards Slievenaglogh (N) from there. If starting from the Silent Valley (see description on page 63), pick up the route from there.

Escape routes: Due to the length of this walk, it is imperative to bail out if necessary. There are several points along the route where this is possible. These are at (1) Silent Valley car park; (2) Hare's Gap – descend north-west to reach the Trassey Track and follow it back to Meelmore Lodge; (3) the col between Slieve Commedagh and Slieve Donard – descend north-east and follow the path to the left of the Glen River back to Donard Forest and Park; (4) the Bog of Donard – descend eastward along a path that links up with the quarry track that runs to the right of Bloody Bridge River. Then follow signs back to Bloody Bridge car park.

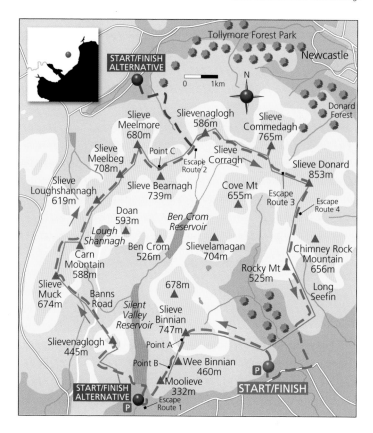

Route Description

Turn left out of the secure car park and follow a broad track steadily uphill to reach a set of gates after around 550m. Enter the metal gate on the right, pass an information board and continue along the track for another 400m until it meets the Mourne Wall.

Leave the track here and go left onto a narrow path running to the right of the wall. Rocky blocks of granite have been put in places to prevent erosion. Ignore all walls running perpendicular to the Mourne Wall and continue uphill toward Slieve Binnian.

The wall ends abruptly as it runs into the vertiginous, rocky crag below the summit of Slieve Binnian. Veer right and away from the wall at a ladder stile before the crag. Follow a narrow, indistinct path steeply uphill, aiming for a gap in a rocky cleft.

95

The steep section of the Mourne Wall from Slieve Binnian down to Wee Binnian, with the Silent Valley Reservoir to the right.

Arrive at a small, flat area on the summit ridge flanked by rocky crags. Head left here to follow a narrow path below the crags, on the Silent Valley side of the ridge. The path crosses a wall and swings around to the opposite (Carrick Little) side of the ridge. On meeting a large tor (Point A), veer left and northward to reach some rocky slabs giving access to the rocky summit of Slieve Binnian (grid ref: **J 320**₆₅ **233**₅₃).

Retrace steps back to Point A and descend south-west from here. A gap between the tor and a large outcrop of rock sits above a steep, rocky gully. Pick a narrow, indistinct path down the gully, then later go right down a steep, grassy slope toward the Mourne Wall when it reappears. A large wedge-shaped boulder sits by the wall at the base of a vertiginous rocky slab.

Keep the Mourne Wall to your right and descend steeply, using your hands where needed, down a rocky slope to the col below. The slope relents, becoming increasingly heathery and grassy closer to the col.

There is a ladder stile at the wall on the col. There are two options here. The **harder option** is to continue south-west and scramble up some rocks to reach the rocky summit of Wee Binnian. From the summit, weave your way down some rock slabs and descend steeply westward (the Silent Valley or western side) to meet a path below. Go left on the path and contour around the base of the rocky summit tor of Wee Binnian to reach its southern ramparts (Point B).

The **easier option** is to cross the ladder stile at the col and follow an indistinct path which flanks the summit of Wee Binnian on the Silent Valley (western) side. The path ends up at Point B, as in the harder option.

With the wall now to your left, descend the grassy slope to reach a boggy saddle with a rusted iron gate at a gap in the wall. Continue south-west and cross a low gap in the wall where it intersects with another.

A gentle rise leads to the broad, grassy and rocky summit of Moolieve (grid ref: **J 312**72 **218**37). Descend a slope south-west, which gets steeper as you reach a ladder stile on the left. Climb over the stile, and now with the wall to your right, go right to descend a moderately steep slope. A narrow path lined with holly and gorse soon reaches another ladder stile at a wall below.

Surmount the stile and turn left onto a distinct path, which is flanked by the wall (left) and some pine trees (right). Reach a junction after around 200m, leave the wall and turn right to descend gently down a forested area to reach a tarmac road below.

You are now at the grounds of the Silent Valley Mountain Park. Turn right on the road and follow it. Pass the Education Centre, Tea Rooms and Visitor Centre on the right. Head between and beyond some granite buildings to reach a large green area. Ascend the concrete steps to the right, which lead to the parapet of the Silent Valley Reservoir.

With the reservoir to your right, walk across a broad tarmac strip on the top of the dam to the opposite end. Go right at a wooden information hut there to follow a trail running close to the reservoir.

The hulking mass of Slievenaglogh (S) now looms ahead. When the trail forks at coloured arrows by a large rock, go right and follow a gravel path (Black Trail) which rises to reach a wooden stile at a fence. Cross the stile and continue beyond a switchback to reach another wooden stile (grid ref: **J 301**94 **220**93).

Do not cross this stile. Instead, head right to follow an informal, grassy and boggy path running to the right of a fence and later a wall. Climb over a ladder stile further uphill, then go right to follow the wall, which is now to your right. Cross an intersecting wall at a low gap and keep following it to reach another ladder stile (grid ref: **J 292**91 **224**13) by a wall.

Cross this stile, turn right and follow the wall to its corner. Turn left at the corner, and with the wall now to your right, ascend steeply uphill towards Slievenaglogh (S). The slope is initially grassy and heathery but becomes increasingly rocky with height. Follow the steep course of the wall, scrambling over some rocky sections where required.

The slope relents nearer the summit. Use a ladder stile to cross the wall, then veer left to reach a small cairn marking the top of Slievenaglogh (S) (grid ref: **J 298**80 **230**22).

Next, with the Mourne Wall to your left, descend north-west from the summit. A steep, informal path gradually relents to meet a broad track by a stout, rusted metal gate and a ladder stile below. The track is known locally as Banns Road.

A section of the Mourne Wall winding its way up to the rocky cairn on Slieve Meelmore.

Cross Banns Road and ascend steeply, following the wall to your left. A stony track runs roughly parallel to the wall, offering a better surface underfoot than the surrounding heather. The track drifts away from the wall and passes through a gap in another wall.

Later, drift back towards the Mourne Wall and follow it up steep, heathery slopes. Climb over a stile to reach a trig point on the broad, grassy summit of Slieve Muck (grid ref: **J 281**14 **249**96). Cross another stile at the wall near the summit.

Now, with the Mourne Wall on your right, descend gently northward on a broad spur to reach a corner where the wall is punctuated by the top of a rocky crag. Go around the crag to the right and descend eastwards to meet the wall again.

A gradual ascent then leads to ladder stile where the wall intersects with another. Climb over the stile to reach a pile of rocks marking the summit of Carn Mountain (grid ref: **J 287**95 **260**13), giving good views of Lough Shannagh below.

Cross the same stile again then with the Mourne Wall to your right, follow it north-east as it rises gently to Point 557m then drops down to a col. Climb over the ladder stile at the col, and now with the Mourne Wall to your left, continue uphill to reach the summit of Slieve Loughshannagh (grid ref: **295**00 **272**03), marked by a pile of rocks.

Drop down to the next col and climb over a ladder stile there. Now, with the wall to your right, ascend a moderately steep slope to reach

The Mourne Wall rising steeply up to Slieve Bearnagh. Its summit tor on the right is an optional scramble.

Slieve Meelbeg (grid ref: **J 300**₇₅ **279**₂₁), whose summit is marked by a large pile of rocks. There are exceptional views here across a large gap toward Slieve Bearnagh in the east, and also along the Mourne Wall which snakes up to the next summit, Slieve Meelmore.

Descend the next slope down to the col, then up again toward Slieve Meelmore. Pass a rocky cairn, then reach a ladder stile before a stone tower at a corner of the Mourne Wall (grid ref: **J 306**₁₁ **287**₇₀) on Slieve Meelmore.

Climb over the stile, then with the wall on your left, descend steeply down to a col at Pollaphuca below. The col sits below the rocky summit of Slieve Bearnagh, and to get there you must ascend steeply up a rocky slope. The path soon drifts away from the Mourne Wall, avoiding some rock slabs. However, maintain a course south-east on the boulder-strewn slope to reach a rocky outcrop by the wall (grid ref: **J 312**₈₇ **280**₇₄, Point C) on the summit plateau.

But the outcrop is not the actual summit. For this, you must veer right and scramble up the rocky summit tor of Slieve Bearnagh, around a 100m away. The easiest line is through a notch at its northern end.

Retrace steps back to Point C. Keep the wall to your left and descend to a gap before rising again to reach Slieve Bearnagh North Tor. Scramble up it if you must, or take the path flanking it on the right, before descending steeply down to Hare's Gap. Some granite steps have been installed along steep sections just before the gap to prevent further erosion.

A large cairn is perched on a flat grassy area of scattered rock to the right of the gap. The Mourne Wall now runs steeply up a flight of granite steps. With the wall now on your left, ascend the steps, then later follow a path that drifts north-east to reach a large cairn near some rock slabs on the summit of Slievenaglogh (N) (grid ref: **J 327**₈₄ **291**₀₆).

The next section simply follows a broad ridge that undulates before rising to reach a small cairn on the next summit, Slieve Corragh (grid ref: **J 337**₁₀ **286**₀₂). Continue along the wall and the section of the ridge towards Slieve Commedagh. This is actually one of the narrowest ridges in

Following the Mourne Wall down to the col below Slieve Commedagh, with Slieve Donard rising ahead.

the area, but the head-height Mourne Wall obstructs the view on the left (northern) side, minimising the exposure.

It is a shame, as the Pot of Legawherry sits behind the wall, so it is worth standing on tiptoe to peer over, or to look back as height is gained to try and catch a glimpse of the pot's rocky and barren recesses. It is also worth looking back at the magnificent Mourne Wall snaking toward Slieve Corragh.

Meet a pipe dispensing clear spring water on the ascent, a useful top-up for your water bottle if needed. Soon, as the slope relents, reach a watchtower whose doorway lintel is carved with the date 1913. There is a ladder stile here too at the southern shoulder of Slieve Commedagh. Climb over the stile, then head north-east to reach the large cairn on the summit of Slieve Commedagh (grid ref: **J 346**14 **286**14) some 250m further along.

Retrace your steps to the wall and watchtower from the summit cairn. Now, with the Mourne Wall to your right, go south-east and descend to a col below. The col is a brief respite before the sting in the tail to complete the Mourne Wall Challenge and the last significant ascent of the day.

So, with the mighty Mourne Wall on your right, climb steeply up towards Slieve Donard – the highest mountain in the Mournes and Northern Ireland. The gradient relents as you reach the Great Carn and trig pillar on the top of a granite tower, marking the summit of Slieve Donard (grid ref: **J 357**98 **276**89).

At once the expansive view of mountains and sea unfolds: its nearby neighbours Slieve Commedagh and Chimney Rock Mountain to the north-west and south-east; the range of peaks across the Annalong Valley as far south as Slieve Binnian; the jagged tors of Slieve Bearnagh in the distance. On a very clear day, even the distant profile of the Wicklow Mountains, the Galloway Hills of Scotland and the Isle of Man can be seen.

Next, descend south-west from Slieve Donard on either side of the Mourne Wall. Aim for the broad saddle on Bog of Donard below. At the Bog of Donard, make sure you are on the west (Annalong) side of the wall. Keep the Mourne Wall to your left and head southwards to Rocky Mountain.

You may choose to go right (south-west) for the short ascent up to the rocky cairn on the broad summit of Rocky Mountain (grid ref: **J 350**55 **252**95), then later regain the wall. However, if you feel you've had enough of ascents at this stage, you may completely bypass the top by simply following the Mourne Wall as it veers south-east for a long, gradual descent towards Long Seefin.

Shortly after Long Seefin, the Mourne Wall intersects another wall to the right. Turn right here to descend on a path leading south-westwards, to the edge of a forest below. At the forest, keep the trees to your left and follow a path to reach a ladder stile beside a gate.

Climb over the stile and turn left along a track flanked by stone walls and trees to reach another gate around 100m away. If the gate is locked, climb over the stone wall to its right with care.

A forest track beyond the gate leads south-east through Dunnywater Forest. It passes an abandoned cottage situated within a granite-walled enclosure under some trees on the left. Not long after, the forest track improves and becomes a lane which later meets Head Road.

Turn right along Head Road and follow it for just over 1.5km to reach the main Carrick Little car park once again. Turn right into the lane, pass the main car park and continue for around 350m to return to your starting point.

A snow-lined Mourne Wall running down the southern slopes of Slieve Donard, as seen from Rocky Mountain.

101

The Western 'Low' Mournes

The Western (Low) Mournes begin where the Eastern (High) Mournes end – emanating westward from the ribbon of road that cuts between Slieve Muck and Pigeon Rock Mountain. The western fringes are marked by a scarp slope extending from the foothills of Rostrevor to a range of low-lying hills north of Spelga Dam.

Eagle Mountain is the highest peak in the Western 'Low' Mournes, one of only two summits that rise above 600m or 2,000ft in the group. The summits are more rounded than their higher counterparts to the east, and are also separated by wider valleys and broader cols. Despite this, a handful of summits such as Hen Mountain, Pierces Castle and Eagle Mountain are graced with elegant tors, rocky outcrops and a line of fierce cliffs. Besides the man-made reservoir of Spelga Dam, natural mountain tarns are tiny and scarce.

The table below lists the 16 peaks of the Western 'Low' Mournes featured in this guidebook, in order of height. Note that all heights are based on the OSNI 1:25,000 *The Mournes Activity Map*.

Mountain Name	Height	Route
Eagle Mountain	638m/2,093ft	18
Shanlieve	626m/2,054ft	18
Slievemoughanmore	559m/1,834ft	18
Pigeon Rock Mountain	534m/1,752ft	16
Cock Mountain	505m/1,657ft	16
Slievenamuck	500m/1,640ft	15
Slievemartin	485m/1,591ft	19
Butter Mountain	480m/1,575ft	15
Spaltha	479m/1,572ft	15
Tievedockaragh	473m/1,552ft	17
Slievemeen	472m/1,549ft	19
Spelga	472m/1,549ft	15
Pierces Castle	465m/1,526ft	17
Rocky Mountain	405m/1,329ft	17
Tornamrock	390m/1,280ft	17
Hen Mountain	354m/1,161ft	16

Spelga, Spaltha, Butter Mountain and Slievenamuck

A straightforward circuit over four tops to the north of Spelga Dam in the Low Mournes.

Grade:	2
Distance:	6km (3¾ miles)
Ascent:	270m (886ft)
Time:	2–2½ hours
Map:	OSNI 1:25,000 *The Mournes Activity Map* or OSNI 1:50,000 Sheet 29

Start/Finish: Large car park at Spelga (grid ref: **J 267**93 **273**08) equipped with picnic tables, litter bins and toilets.

Getting there: From Newcastle: Follow directions from Newcastle to Bryansford along the Bryansford Road (B180). Pass the Barbican Gate entrance of Tollymore Forest before reaching a T-junction. Turn left here along the B180 towards Hilltown, passing the gates of Tollymore Forest and later its Mountain Centre (both on the left). When the forest ends, the Trassey Valley opens up on the left. Pass Tullyree Road junction on the right and approximately 1.6km (1 mile) afterwards, turn left into Slievenaman Road. Continue for about 4km (2½ miles) to pass Fofanny Dam and some forestry on your left. When the forest ends, drive another 2km (1¼ miles) to reach a junction on the right (signposted B27, Hilltown). Turn right here, and reach Spelga Dam car park after just over 1.2km (¾ mile) on your left. **From Kilkeel:** Take the Moyad Road (B27) out of Kilkeel. After just over 13km (8 miles), the B27 goes left at a junction toward Spelga Dam. Follow the B27 and after just over 1.2km (¾ mile) reach Spelga Dam car park on your left. **From Hilltown:** Take the road east out of Hilltown. Ignore the B8 (Rathfriland) junction and bear right onto the B27. After around 1.5km (1 mile), ignore the B180 (Dundrum/Newcastle) and turn right onto the B27 towards Kilkeel. Follow the road uphill to the Spelga Pass. After approximately 1.2km (¾ mile) after a sharp bend, the road cuts through the narrow pass, flanked by hills on both sides, to reach Spelga Dam car park on your right.

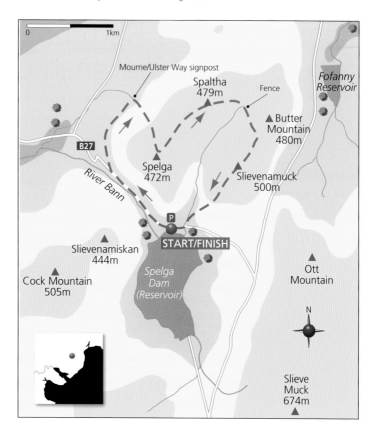

S pelga Dam is located on an elevated plain between the High (Eastern) and Low (Western) Mournes. The 345m (¼-mile) long concrete dam was constructed between 1954–57 by the Portadown and Banbridge Joint Waterworks Board. The dam, which once supplied water for the mills along the mighty River Bann nearby, is a sizeable water catchment area of 705 hectares (1,740 acres). Today, it supplies water to both Banbridge and Portadown.

It is interesting to note that this vast, flat area was once covered in a sheet of ice surrounded by glaciers and peaks. When the ice age ended around 10,000 years ago, the glaciers retreated and the area was transformed into a wide, upland valley. This area, where Spelga Dam sits today, was once called Deers' Meadow. In bygone days, its grassy upland plains were used by cowherds, who drove their cattle up in the mountains for summer grazing in a practice known as booleying.

This is by far the easiest route in all the mountains of Mourne. Parts of the route run along the Mourne Way, a 38km (23½-mile) long-distance walking trail starting from the sea at Newcastle to the scenic village of Rostrevor at Carlingford Lough in the south.

Signboard near the ladder stile and Mourne/ Ulster Way signpost – leave the road here at grid ref. J 260₁₄ 280₃₄.

Route Description

Turn left out of the car park. With Spelga Dam away to your left, walk down the B27 for around 300m. Use the soft verge on the left of the road to reach a small lane at the entrance of the dam building. There is a 'magic road' on a short section of a surfaced driveway entrance to the dam building here, where a car can apparently roll uphill.

This is where the soft verge ends – for the next stretch of around 650m, take care while walking down the B27. If needed, use a narrow grassy strip to the right of the road. The B27 now runs above the River Bann, which flows along a deep, rocky ravine. A sturdy stone wall borders the B27, shielding passing traffic from the steep drop to the riverbed below.

Follow the road further downhill past the end of the wall. Leave the B27 before a sharp bend by climbing over a ladder stile at a signboard and signpost for the Mourne/Ulster Way (grid ref: **J 260**₁₄ **280**₃₄) on the right.

Follow an indistinct, grassy path that runs alongside a wall and fence to the left. There are great views over the wall toward the brown twin tops of Hen Mountain. Continue along the path until reaching the next Mourne/Ulster Way signpost around 900m away.

It is now time to drift away from the wall and ascend the moderately steep slope to the right. The slope consists mainly of short grass with the odd rocky patch. Keep heading south-east until reaching the brow of the hill. Pass a small tarn just before the summit of Spelga (grid ref: **J 264**₉₃ **281**₀₃), which is marked by a small pile of rocks.

The summit overlooks Spelga Dam, which is now spread below to the south. The mountains of the High and Low Mournes can also be distinguished from here, with Slieve Croob also visible much further north.

Spelga Dam at sunset.

Go along the grassy mountain plateau for around 700m toward the next top – Spaltha – away in the north-east. This is an easy stretch where you can relax and appreciate the contrasting landscape of lowlands on the left and the higher mountains of Mourne farther away to the right.

After a slight rise, reach the unmarked top of Spaltha (grid ref: **J 270**$_{53}$ **287**$_{07}$), no more than a grassy strip on a clump of rocks. Views here include the distant Lough Island Reavy Reservoir below the slopes of Slievenalargy away to the north-east. This man-made lake is popular for fishing pike, perch and wild brown trout.

From Spaltha, head eastward to meet a fence. Turn right at the fence and follow it gradually uphill. It is best to keep the fence on your left to avoid crossing it later on Butter Mountain, where it is lined with awkward strips of barbed wire. However, there are some rather boggy sections early on, so it is recommended to cross the fence onto its opposite (drier) side, then cross it again (once past the bog) at the earliest opportunity. Whatever you do, do not leave it too late!

Turn right at a Mourne/Ulster Way signpost at the top of a broad spur on the upper slopes of Butter Mountain, which inherited its name from the practice of preserving butter by burying it in cool upland bogs. The Mourne Way reaches its highest point here.

Follow an informal path across the broad, grassy ridge to reach the unmarked summit of Slievenamuck. From here, the distinctive tops of Slieve Bearnagh and Slieve Binnian appear small and insignificant farther away to the east/south-east. Soon after, Spelga Dam, its car park, a ribbon of road and a patch of trees come into full view below.

A grassy slope leads comfortably downhill toward the dam on a vague, trodden path. Aim for a sheep's pen and a distinct track below. Veer left on reaching the track and continue, to meet a gate by the B27. Go through the gate, turn right on the road and head back to the car park at the start.

Hen Mountain, Cock Mountain and Pigeon Rock Mountain

One of the most popular circuits in the Low Mournes, known colloquially as the 'birdie walk'.

Grade:	3
Distance:	10.5km (6½ miles)
Ascent:	580m (1,903ft)
Time:	3½–4½ hours
Map:	OSNI 1:25,000 *The Mournes Activity Map*

Start/Finish: Sandbank Road car park and picnic area (grid ref: **233**14 **277**41), north of Rocky River Bridge. There are spaces for around 12 cars.

Getting there: From Newcastle: Follow directions from Newcastle to Bryansford along the Bryansford Road (B180). Pass the Barbican Gate entrance of Tollymore Forest before reaching a T-junction. Turn left here along the B180 towards Hilltown. Ignore all minor side-roads and follow the B180 until reaching the Kilkeel Road (B27) junction. Turn left with care into the B27, then at a crossroads 450m further on, turn right onto Sandbank Road. The car park is on the right just over 1.2km (¾ mile) ahead.

From Kilkeel: Take the Moyad Road (B27) out of Kilkeel. After just over 13km (8 miles), the B27 veers left at a junction toward Spelga Dam. Go left here and follow the B27 through Spelga Pass. After a sharp bend, the road dips down into the Glenaveagh Valley. Approximately 2.5km (1½ miles) after the bend, arrive at a crossroads. Turn left here onto Sandbank Road. The car park is on the right just over 1.2km (¾ mile) ahead. **From Hilltown:** Take the road east out of Hilltown. Ignore the B8 (Rathfriland) junction and bear right onto the B27. After around 1.5km (1 mile), ignore the B180 (Dundrum/Newcastle) at the next junction and stay on the B27 by turning right in the direction of Kilkeel. At a crossroads 450m further along, turn right onto Sandbank Road. The car park is on the right just over 1.2km (¾ mile) ahead.

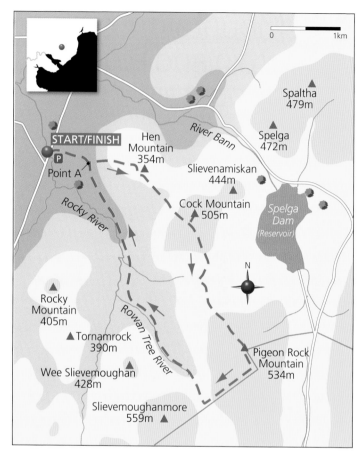

n this area of the Low (Western Mournes), several of the mountaintops are named for birds. This route describes a circuit of three of them. First is a distinctive top known as Hen Mountain, whose rocky peak is crowned with a collection of granite tors. Next is the rounded twin-topped Cock Mountain, followed by the broad-shouldered Pigeon Rock Mountain. One more summit, Eagle Mountain, the highest of the 'bird' tops is described in Route 18.

Hen Mountain is by far the most interesting of all these tops. Its summit is adorned by a collection of four granite tors: West Tor, the Tower, Summit Tor and South Tor. An obvious path leads walkers up to the Summit Tor from the west, but all the other tors require some scrambling to reach the top. There are some sheltered spots between these tors, but the bare rock is exposed to the wind in all directions. All the tors are popular with rock

Climbers on the Tower tor on Hen Mountain.

climbers, and have climbing route names such as High Noon, Asterisk and Touchdown.

Route Description

Leave the car park and cross Sandbank Road to meet a broad track directly opposite. The track is just to the left of a house. When the track forks around 100m further, head left, then go through a metal gate. After a slight rise, the track reaches another metal gate. Use a smaller metal gate to its right (Point A) to enter the open mountainside.

Hen Mountain now rises to the left. Leave the track here and ascend a moderately steep, grassy slope towards it. An indistinct, trodden path helps somewhat as the incline steepens near the top. A well-trodden path later passes two medium-sized granite tors on the grassy summit plateau of Hen Mountain before heading towards the large Summit Tor (grid ref: **J 245**₂₇ **276**₁₃).

The Summit Tor is a monstrous slab of bare granite, and the way up it from the summit plateau is obvious. All the other tors may be appreciated from its top, as well as expansive views of the surrounding area, which include patchwork fields and low-lying hills to the west and north, a pudding-shaped collection of rounded, brown hills to the south, and the nearby Cock Mountain to the south-east.

Next, scramble down a small gully with care, using some rock steps, to gain the col between the Summit Tor and South Tor. If you are uncomfortable with this, then retrace your steps to the grassy plateau, flank the Summit Tor on the Rocky River (southern) side and contour along the hillside to reach the aforementioned col.

Once at the col, flank the South Tor to the right, on the Rocky River (southern) side. Once the rocky South Tor is completely bypassed, go left and uphill again, aiming for a broad col between Hen and Cock Mountain.

This col is notoriously boggy and the trodden path leading towards Cock Mountain is badly eroded. The ascent is a bit arduous as the slope steepens with height – but if it is any consolation the ground gets drier. Soon enough, Cock Mountain's twin tops are reached. A small cairn is perched on a large rocky outcrop to the right, but the top marked on the map as the summit is the one with the larger cairn on the left (grid ref: **J 253**57 **268**43).

There are good views back to Hen Mountain from the large cairn. Other views also include the nearer, lower outlier of Slievenamiskan and the large, rounded summit of Pigeon Rock Mountain farther away to the south-east. Spelga Dam can also be seen in its entirety to the east, with the mountains of the High Mournes as the backdrop.

From the summit, descend a grassy slope toward a large col 800m away to the south-east. Aim for a broad, grassy track on the col below. The track goes right, rising gradually to reach a broad shoulder. Once there, go left and head south-east towards Pigeon Rock Mountain.

Ascend the moderately steep, grassy slope to reach a wall with a ladder stile at its corner. A small pile of rocks nearby marks the broad and

Looking south-west from Point 505m on Cock Mountain toward its twin summit.

Spelga Dam and the landscape to the east from Cock Mountain.

The view north-east from the summit of Pigeon Rock Mountain, with Slieve Bearnagh and its surrounding hills visible in the distance.

hummocky summit of Pigeon Rock Mountain (grid ref: **J 261**31 **250**29). A look back at Cock Mountain from here reveals the extent of the bare and barren landscape separating the two tops. There are also good views to the north-east of the higher Eastern Mournes, with the bristly tors of Slieve Bearnagh looking especially prominent, even from afar. Slievemoughanmore rises proudly in the opposite direction, with its lower outlier of Wee Slievemoughan to its right. The wide valley of Rowan Tree River sweeps in front of Wee Slievemoughan, and on a clear day the broad track meandering near the river is discernible from here.

From the summit, keep the wall to your left and follow it to reach a col below Slivemoughanmore. Once at the col, turn right to follow a stream flowing north-west. The stream is the source of the Rowan Tree River and cuts through a deep gorge on its way down the valley.

The descent gets quite steep and the ground can be fairly slippery, especially on or after a wet day, so take care. Drift away from the stream to avoid boggy areas, heading back to it later where the ground is drier. The broad track can once again be seen in the wide valley below.

Descend to meet the track (grid ref: **J 250**18 **248**98) running beside the Rowan Tree River. The track is rocky, stony and pebbly, and provides a comfortable descent back to base. All the tors on Hen Mountain look particular impressive from this southerly direction.

Follow the track back to the gate at Point A, and from here simply retrace your steps back to the car park.

Rocky Mountain, Tornamrock, Pierces Castle and Tievedockaragh

Batt's Wall, Castle Bog and a rugged round of low-lying hills close to Leitrim Lodge.	**Grade:**	3
	Distance:	8.5km (5¼ miles)
	Ascent:	485m (1,591ft)
	Time:	3–3¾ hours
	Map:	OSNI 1:25,000 *The Mournes Activity Map* or OSNI 1:50,000 Sheet 29

Start/Finish: Leitrim Lodge car park (grid ref: **J 224**33 **255**62).

Getting there: From Newcastle: Follow directions from Newcastle to Bryansford along the Bryansford Road (B180). Pass the Barbican Gate entrance of Tollymore Forest before reaching a T-junction. Turn left here along the B180 towards Hilltown. Ignore all minor side roads and follow the B180 until reaching the Kilkeel Road (B27) junction. Turn left with care onto the B27, and at the crossroads 450m further on, turn right onto Sandbank Road. Continue along this road for around 3.5km (2¼ miles) to reach Leitrim Lodge car park on the left in a shaded area. **From Kilkeel:** Take the Moyad Road (B27) out of Kilkeel. After just over 13km (8 miles), the B27 veers left at a junction toward Spelga Dam. Go left here and follow the B27 through Spelga Pass. After a sharp bend, the road dips down into the Glenaveagh Valley. Approximately 2.5km (1½ miles) after the bend, arrive at a crossroads. Turn left here onto Sandbank Road. Continue along this road for around 3.5km (2¼ miles) to reach Leitrim Lodge car park on the left in a shaded area. **From Hilltown:** Take the road east out of Hilltown. Ignore the B8 (Rathfriland) junction and bear right onto the B27. After around 1.5km (1 mile), ignore the B180 (Dundrum/Newcastle) and turn right onto the B27 in the direction of Kilkeel. At a crossroads 450m further on, turn right onto Sandbank Road. Continue along this road for around 3.5km (2¼ miles) to reach Leitrim Lodge car park on the left in a shaded area.

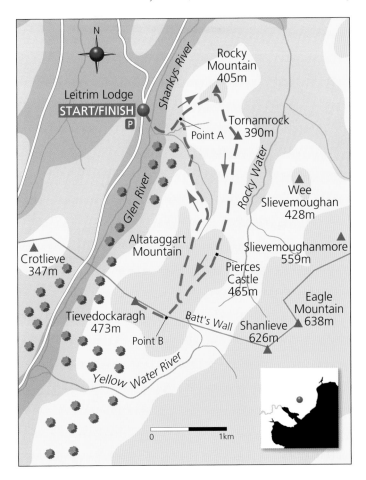

'Heavily loaded
From Pierce's bogs,
Wi' a cart o' peat
The oul' mare jogs.'
– 'Cartin' Peat' by Richard Rowley (1877–1947)

The area around Leitrim Lodge was known as Batt's Estate. Now managed by trustees, it was owned by a wealthy landowner, Narcissus Batt, in 1834. Batt built a series of drystone walls in straight lines across the mountains to mark his estate. The woods and foothills of Leitrim Lodge also became the lands north of Winterfell where Bran first

The Mourne Way/Ulster Way/St Patrick's Way signpost at the start of the walk, with Rocky Mountain rising in the background.

meets Jojen and Meera in the epic TV series *Game of Thrones*.

This route begins from Leitrim Lodge car park and visits four low-lying hills to the east and south: Rocky Mountain, which provides the best views; Tornamrock and Pierces Castle, both graced by rocky outcrops; and the rounded, featureless top of Tievedockaragh which runs close to Batt's Wall.

A flat, peaty area known as Castle Bog is crossed midway through the route. It lies below the south-western slopes of Pierces Castle and measures around 500m x 500m. Turf cutting used to be common here in the past, evidenced by a complex network of old bog roads that scar the area. Over the summer months, turf or peat was cut from bog by hand, using a two-sided spade called a *sleán*. The dried turf was then loaded onto carts and pulled by horses from Castle Bog to Hilltown. Peat or turf taken from the bog was an important source of fuel for heating and cooking in the local dwellings at the time. Care must be taken when crossing Castle Bog in thick mist as the terrain is featureless and good navigation skills are required.

Route Description

Take a tarmac path near some information boards on the southern end of the car park. The path leads south-east and a swinging metal gate provides access to the open countryside. Cross a concrete bridge spanning Shankys River then follow a broad gravel track beyond.

The track passes close to the trees of Batt's Wood and forks around 200m further. The trees in these woods were planted during the lifetime of Narcissus Batt, making them nearly two centuries old. Scots pine were extensively planted but today holly and rowan trees have thrived amongst the sheltering pines.

Veer left at the fork and follow the track to a wooden signpost marking the Mourne Way/Ulster Way/St Patrick's Way. Leave the track around 50m beyond this signpost at a large boulder (grid ref: **J 228**74 **255**70, Point A) to follow an informal, grassy path that rises up a moderately steep slope

The panorama to the north-east from the summit of Rocky Mountain includes Hen and Cock Mountains in the midground.

towards Rocky Mountain. Go to the right of a jumble of boulders higher upslope, then zigzag steeply uphill on grass to pass some outcrops of rock. The slope finally relents as you approach the summit, the top of which is marked by a rocky cairn (grid ref: **J 233**₈₅ **258**₅₇).

The rest of the circuit from here to Tornamrock, Pierces Castle and Tievedockaragh may be fully appreciated from the summit on a clear day. The most impressive panorama unfolds to the east/north-east, with the distant peaks of the High (Eastern) Mournes peeping behind the closer neighbours of Hen and Cock Mountains. Farther to the south, Carlingford Lough and the hills of the Cooley Peninsula supplement the vista, and beyond the green plains to the far north lie Slieve Croob and the Dromara hills.

When ready to depart, descend roughly south-east along an earthen path to a col below, then continue uphill towards Tornamrock. Pass an undercut granite outcrop just before the broad, grassy and unmarked top of Tornamrock which is peppered with rocks and boulders.

From here, continue southwards along a broad ridge to Pierces Castle. This is an enjoyable stretch, giving lingering views of Slievemoughanmore and Eagle Mountain rising above Rocky Water River ahead to the south-east. Soon, pass an area of scattered rock before reaching a col. Beyond this, a path leads comfortably uphill to reach a rocky tor on Pierces Castle (grid ref: **J 233**₉₁ **239**₂₉).

Descend on bare rock from the rocky slab of Pierces Castle to reach a broad gritted track on an extensive area of peat and heather. This is the flat area of Castle Bog where paths proliferate, including an old bog road. Use

The location where Batt's Wall meets the fence at Point B.

the paths or road if you wish, but aim roughly south-west. At some stage, you should come across an earthen path that gradually rises towards Batt's Wall, meeting it at a point where it joins a fence (grid ref: **J 226**₆₁ **230**₈₄, Point B).

Cross the low fence, turn right and follow an eroded path to reach a small pile of rocks on the broad top of Tievedockaragh (grid ref: **J 223**₀₈ **232**₃₄), a featureless oasis of grass and heather. From here, there are extended views over all the hills of the Low Mournes, including the rounded backs of Leckan More and Slieve Roosley further to the south-west. The distant peaks of the High Mournes are also discernible much farther away to the north-east.

Retrace steps from Tievedockaragh back to Point B, keeping an eye along the soggy areas here for bog asphodel, with its distinctive yellow flower in the summer months. From Point B, retrace your steps along the path taken up to Batt's Wall earlier for around 250m. At this point, leave the path for a rugged patch of grass and heather in the direction of Altataggart Mountain, roughly due north.

Persevere through the heather to reach a broad track (grid ref: **J 228**₈₂ **233**₇₃). The track is intermittent with boggy sections, and after around 500m, it reaches a junction (grid ref: **J 230**₂₇ **238**₃₉) below the eastern slopes of Altataggart Mountain.

Follow the broad track here for over 1km as it descends initially north-eastwards, later veering northwestwards. After crossing a stream, the track runs above a gorge (on the left) and passes a water service reservoir before reaching the boulder at Point A.

Retrace steps from there back to the start.

Slievemoughanmore, Eagle Mountain and Shanlieve

A quiet and picturesque valley in the Low Mournes bordered by three peaks and a Great Gully.

From Community Centre		From top of Sandy Brae Road	
Grade:	3	**Grade:**	3
Distance:	14km (8¾ miles)	**Distance:**	10.5km (6½ miles)
Ascent:	710m (2,329ft)	**Ascent:**	660m (2,165ft)
Time:	4¾–5¾ hours	**Time:**	3½–4½ hours

MAP: OSNI 1:25,000 *The Mournes Activity Map* or OSNI 1:50,000 Sheet 29

Start/Finish: Lay-by on the left at the top of Sandy Brae Road, before the farm building (grid ref: **J 263**82 **205**11). If there are no spaces here, do not park directly opposite or at the farm building. Instead use the parking spaces at the Cnocnafeola Community Centre along Tullyframe Road (grid ref: **J 268**07 **189**34).

Getting there: Best approached from Kilkeel. Take the Moyad Road (B27) out of Kilkeel. After around 6.5km (4 miles), turn left onto Attical Bog Road. Follow the road into Attical village. Pass The Mourne Lodge (themournelodge.com) on the right, before reaching a crossroads with a church on the right. Continue ahead there for just over 1km (0.6 mile) before turning right onto Sandy Brae Road. This road is narrow and potholed, gradually turning from tarmac to gravel further uphill. If you choose to park at the community centre, drive past Sandy Brae Road for around 200m, to reach the buildings on your right.

This route follows a snaking path along and above the Windy Gap River, passing beneath the eastern flanks of Eagle Mountain, the highest peak in the Low Mournes. From afar, the mountain appears as a tame, rounded dome with a long, gentle crest. But this is deceiving as there are actually some sheer crags and rocky pinnacles all

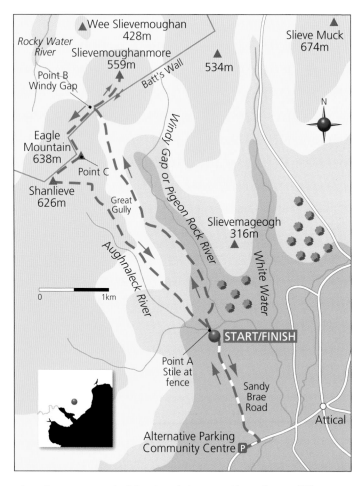

along its eastern end, giving it real character. These fierce cliff lines can be best appreciated as you walk up the quiet, barren valley toward the boggy col of Windy Gap.

Windy Gap, as the name suggests, can be notoriously windy, and is especially exposed to cold north-west winds funnelling up from the Rocky Water Valley. Tucked below the steep slopes of Slievemoughanmore, Windy Gap was shaped nearly 12,000 years ago during the ice age, when a torrent of meltwater escaped from a retreating glacier. Slievemoughanmore, our first peak of call, is a summit consisting of a 'roof' of ancient Silurian shale capping an igneous bedrock of granite, which forms the bulk of the mountain.

The view towards the Eastern (High) Mournes from the summit of Eagle Mountain.

The next section of the route from Slievemoughanmore to Eagle Mountain and ultimately to Shanlieve is straightforward, as it follows the course of Batt's Wall, a useful guide in the mist. The wall, built by Narcissus Batt in the nineteenth century to mark his estate, reaches its highest points on the slope of Eagle Mountain and Shanlieve.

Route Description

From the top of the Sandy Brae Road, pass the farm buildings on the right and follow the road across a footbridge over the Aughnaleck River. If the river is in spate after or on a wet day, use the raised concrete bridge on the left.

Turn left immediately after the river onto a grassy path that runs alongside it. The path is flanked by a stone wall on the right, and soon swings around to meet a stile by a fence (Point A) at the corner of some trees.

Cross the stile and follow the stone wall and fence to its corner. Veer right there, and right again around the next corner 50m further. From here, keep following the wall and fence to reach a broad, distinct track.

Turn left along this track, which heads roughly north-west into the mountains. The track initially runs along the Windy Gap or Pigeon Rock River, which is away to its right. After passing a metal bridge (don't cross it), the track crosses a tiny stream. Bear left at a fork immediately after the stream as the track now runs alongside a stone wall on the right.

Continue for around 750m to reach another fork. Veer left here to follow a track that soon veers away from the wall and snakes uphill. Slabs of granite are embedded in sections along the track as a prevention to further erosion.

Looking north at the cliffs of Eagle Mountain from the top of Great Gully.

The track soon meanders under the sheer cliffs of Great Gully, the most extensive and impressive crag in the Low Mournes. Its north-east-facing aspect exposes it to weather elements drifting in from the Irish Sea, resulting in vegetation and grass clinging to almost every ledge. The crag is a haunt of rock climbers and includes technical routes such as Honest To God, Fanta and Musical Cracks.

The track makes a beeline for the col of Windy Gap, which can be clearly seen in the distance. Around 150m before the gap, the track takes a sudden turn uphill and left. Here, leave the comfort of the track and aim for the prominent wall on your right. Follow the wall as it contours below the steep slope to your left.

The wall intersects another wall running perpendicular to it at Windy Gap. Two ladder stiles are found here (Point B). Climb over the stile in front of you to access the gap on the Rocky Water (northern) side.

Next, veer right and with the wall now on your right, ascend the moderately steep slope in the direction of Slievemoughanmore. After roughly 400m reach a small tarn (it might be dry during hot summer months), then head left and away from the wall. Finally arrive at a pile of rocks on a grassy, granite outcrop after a small rise. There are fine views here back towards Windy Gap and the whaleback-shaped Eagle Mountain, which can be seen rising to the south-west.

The true summit of Slievemoughanmore (grid ref: **J 249**$_{82}$ **241**$_{32}$) is actually around 100m away to the right, and its top is marked by a larger pile of rocks. Despite being only 100m away, the surrounding views are even more extensive from here and include Eagle Mountain again to the south-west, Rocky Mountain to the north-west, Hen Mountain and Cock Mountain to the north and Spelga Dam to the north-east. The mountains of the High Mournes can also be seen to the right of Spelga Dam, with the bristly top of Slieve Bearnagh looking especially prominent.

Retrace steps from the summit back to Windy Gap at Point B. Once back at the gap, keep the wall to your left and follow it in the opposite direction toward Eagle Mountain. The slope is steep to begin with and later relents as it approaches the point where the wall turns a corner. The vast, barren landscape of the Rocky Water Valley and its surrounding hills sweeps away to your right, with the rocky outcrop of Pierces Castle clearly visible.

When the wall eventually turns a corner, the shimmering waters of Carlingford Lough and the masts of Black Mountain/Clermont Cairn away on the Cooley Peninsula can be seen on a clear day. Veer left at the corner of the wall, and not long after even the profile of the hummocky ridge of Slieve Foye, also on the Cooley Peninsula, can be distinguished.

Climb over a ladder stile at the next corner of the wall (Point C), then continue ahead for around 100m to reach a large cairn marking the summit of Eagle Mountain (grid ref: **J 244**$_{90}$ **229**$_{75}$). The summit is the highest point in all of the Low (Western) Mournes and provides exceptional 360-degree views of the surrounding area as far as the Cooley Peninsula. The wave of High Mourne peaks to the east/north-east are the most intriguing, with the crinkly tops of Slieve Bearnagh on one end and Slieve Binnian on the other.

When ready, retrace steps back to the corner of the wall at Point C from the summit. Go left here, and now with the wall to your right, follow it up a gradual rise to its next corner. Leave the wall at the corner, veer left and after around 50m, reach the cairn on the summit of Shanlieve (grid ref: **J 240**$_{72}$ **226**$_{67}$). Views across Carlingford Lough over to the Cooley Peninsula are even closer (and better) from here.

The next 500m or so descends roughly eastward across trackless, rugged moorland. Arrive at the top of sheer cliffs that line the eastern flanks of Eagle Mountain, giving extensive views across the Windy Gap Valley and vertigo-inducing glimpses down into the Great Gully.

Here, keep well away from the cliff edge and follow an indistinct path south-east down the spur. After around 1.3km, the path veers right, dropping away from the spine of the spur. At this point, leave the path and maintain a course on the trackless, grassy spur. A few hundred metres later, a vague path soon materialises, becoming more distinct as height is lost.

Some trees and the farm building at the top of the Sandy Brae Road soon come into view. Simply descend the rest of the spur, aiming for the stile at the corner of the trees (Point A). Retrace steps from here back to the start.

Cloughmore Stone, Slievemeen and Slievemartin

An exhilarating circuit around the woods and hills of Rostrevor overlooking Carlingford Lough in an area that C.S.Lewis thought of as 'his idea of Narnia'.

Grade:	3
Distance:	9km (5½ miles)
Ascent:	510m (1,673ft)
Time:	3–4 hours
Map:	OSNI 1:25,000 *The Mournes Activity Map*, OSNI 1:50,000 Sheet 29 or OSi 1:50,000 Sheet 36

Start/Finish: Main car park at Kilbroney Forest Park (grid ref: **J 186**₆₀ **179**₈₉). Note: if the main car park is closed due to ice in the winter months, park at the large lay-by on the right (grid ref: **J 185**₄₄ **177**₅₀) just after the ranger's building at the forest park's entrance.

Getting there: The entrance of Kilbroney Forest Park is around 1km (0.6 mile) after the Kilkeel junction at Rostrevor. Leave the A2 and turn left into the forest park. Drive by the ranger's building on the right, pass a large lay-by and continue to reach a fork in the road. Go right there and after around 75m arrive at the main car park on the left.

Kilbroney Forest Park has number of facilities, including a camping/caravan site, playground, tennis courts, café, the Cloughmore Centre and mountain-bike trails. It also has two waymarked walks – the easier Narnia Trail and the harder Cloughmore Trail. The main car park is opened at 9 a.m. throughout the year. Closing times vary: Nov.–Mar. (5 p.m.), Apr. (7 p.m.), May (9 p.m.), June–Aug. (10 p.m.), Sept. (9 p.m.), Oct. (7 p.m.). For up-to-date car park opening times call +44 (0)28 417 38134.

Rostrevor is an idyllic village situated around 5km (3 miles) from Warrenpoint along the scenic A2 coast road. The two rounded tops of Slievemeen and Slievemartin rise high above its woodlands to the south-east, overlooking the beautiful Carlingford Lough.

In ancient times, Rostrevor was called *Caisleann Rhuadhri,* named after a castle founded by one of the Lords of Iveagh, Rory Magenniss. The

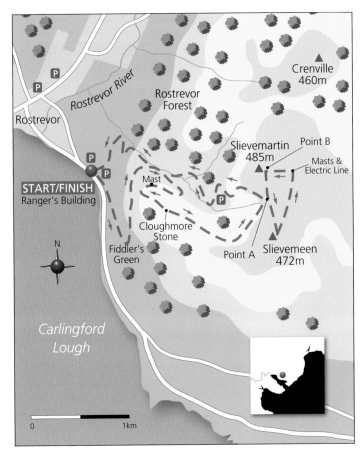

baronial castle, of which there is now no longer any trace, was subsequently occupied by the Trevor family, who later renamed it *Caisleann Trevor*.

Sir Edward Trevor was a Welsh settler in the area in the early 17th century. While it is generally believed that 'Trevor' is derived from Edward's surname, there is some debate over the first component, 'Ros'. One theory suggests that it is derived from the name of Edward's wife, Rose, a daughter of Henry Ussher, Archbishop of Armagh. However, other claims suggest that Edward Trevor simply adopted the Irish word *ros* meaning 'wood', as it befitted the area.

Besides Slievemeen and Slievemartin, this route visits the popular Cloughmore Stone (*Cloch Mór*, 'big stone') high above the woodlands of Kilbroney Forest Park. Legend suggests that the mythical warrior Fionn MacCumhaill was hunting on Slieve Foye one day when he was faced

Cloughmore Trail signpost.

with Ruscaire, a giant of ice and winter. A fierce battle ensued between the pair, lasting three days and three nights. Finally, in a fit of anger, Fionn picked up a boulder and hurled it across the lough. It landed on Ruscaire's head, killing him. The boulder, as you have probably guessed, is the Cloughmore Stone.

Route Description

From the main car park, walk back along the road towards the large lay-by near the entrance. After passing the ranger's building, leave the road and veer left into a lane. Pass another building then shortly veer left again onto a path signposted 'Forest Nature Reserve and Fiddler's Green'.

When the path meets a broad gravel track, turn left and follow it gradually uphill into the trees of the National Nature Reserve. Carlingford Lough can be seen through gaps in the trees on the right. Many of the trees here are what remains of an ancient natural oak woodland that once clothed the lower slopes of the Mournes several centuries ago. Sadly, most of the oak trees were felled in the eighteenth and nineteenth centuries for use in the shipbuilding industry.

Today, the forest is a Special Area of Conservation with around 1,000 hectares (2,471 acres) of planted trees that include the Douglas fir, European larch, Lodgepole pine and Sitka spruce. Ash, hazel, holly and willow also grow abundantly and there is a rich carpet of bluebells, ferns, grass and woodrush on the woodland floor.

At a fork higher uphill, go left, following signs for Fiddler's Green. A flat, grassy clearing is soon reached on the left, with a bench and a Fiddler's Green signpost nearby. The green was once a hub for local entertainment and this practice is maintained in the annual Fiddler's Green traditional music festival.

From Fiddler's Green, continue to follow the track uphill to meet a T-junction. Turn left here along a forest track that soon levels after a slight rise. There are glimpses over Carlingford Lough to the left. The track meanders under a dense canopy of tall conifers on the right before reaching a T-junction soon after a forest barrier.

Turn right at the T-junction onto a broad, surfaced forestry road. After passing a broad lay-by, reach a track signposted 'Cloughmore Trail' on the right. Leave the road here and follow a track uphill. The track runs beneath some tall conifers and soon reaches a T-junction.

Rostrevor Forest.

This is where you momentarily leave the Cloughmore Trail by turning right onto a narrow path. The path meets a broad forest track after a slight rise. Turn right here and follow the track, which passes under a mast to reach a circular viewing area. Veer left onto a path before the viewing area and ascend uphill, ignoring subsidiary mountain-bike trails running perpendicular to it.

The path meets up with a T-junction ahead, and here the fabled Cloughmore Stone is now visible on a rise to the right. Turn right here to finally reach the giant boulder (grid ref: **J 191**$_{60}$ **172**$_{61}$). Despite legendary tales of how it got here, the Cloughmore Stone is really an 'erratic' – a boulder dislodged from the mountains during the ice age and deposited in its present location as the glacier receded. It is thought that the 50-tonne boulder provided Belfast novelist C.S. Lewis with the inspiration for Aslan's table in his *Chronicles of Narnia*. Some local folk also suggest that walking around the Cloughmore Stone seven times will allegedly bring good luck!

From here, it is easy to see why C.S. Lewis once said, 'that part of Rostrevor which overlooks Carlingford Lough is my idea of Narnia'. There are stunning vistas down to Carlingford Lough and across it to the hills of the Cooley Peninsula, with the scenic coast road connecting Rostrevor and Warrenpoint also apparent. See if you can spot a 30m (100ft) granite obelisk on the road. It is dedicated to Major General Robert Ross of Bladensburg, a Rostrevor native who fought in the American War of Independence. Major Ross's troops set fire to all public buildings in Washington during the war and their actions inspired the writing of the national anthem 'Star-Spangled Banner'.

From the Cloughmore Stone, the tops of Slievemeen and Slievemartin are clearly visible to the distant east. Descend to an obvious track from the stone and go right, in the direction of Slievemeen. The track initially contours along the hillside above the lovely, large wooded valley of Cloughmore Glen, then later giving fine views towards Rostrevor as it turns a corner and heads north-east. Ignore all subsidiary paths running perpendicular to the main track along this section as they are all mountain-bike trails.

The track finally comes to a halt at a ladder stile by a fence (grid ref: **J 202**$_{00}$ **173**$_{50}$) above the forest at Point A. The rugged, open mountain lies waiting beyond the fence. Some transmitter masts can now be seen protruding ahead, with Slievemartin rising prominently to the left.

Climb over the stile and turn right to follow a low stone wall. A grassy slope leads to the broad, unmarked top of Slievemeen (purists: note that the actual summit is guarded by a barbed-wire fence). There are good views from here along the Knockshee ridge to the south-east and also across Carlingford Lough towards the Cooley Peninsula.

From Slievemeen, head roughly north-east towards the transmission masts you saw earlier. A path soon peters out, giving way to rough, grassy terrain all the way until reaching the masts (grid ref: **J 204**$_{18}$ **176**$_{08}$).

At the masts, views suddenly open up to the low-lying hills in the north. But we are heading west, towards a ladder stile at a fence (Point B). Cross the ladder stile and continue for another 100m to finally reach the summit trig pillar of Slievemartin (grid ref: **J 201**$_{17}$ **176**$_{48}$).

The summit area is graced by a profusion of bilberry, crowberry, grass, heather and woodrush. However, it is the surrounding views that are more intoxicating, dominated by the rugged crest of Slieve Foye across Carlingford Lough to the south and the expanse of the Low Mournes in the opposite direction.

Retrace steps back to the fence at Point B from the summit. Turn right and follow the fence down back to the ladder stile at the top of the forest at Point A. Here, two tracks emanate to the right of the stile. Ignore the (marked) mountain-bike track; instead, take the one to the left of it.

The track drops steeply down the pine forest under the canopy of tall trees via a series of switchbacks to emerge finally at the Cloughmore upper car park. Turn right here and walk the length of the car park toward the exit road running downhill. Follow the forest drive down to reach a bridge spanning across the Glen Stream.

Turn left here and cross the bridge, then continue to follow the road downhill for around 500m. After a switchback, pass a house on the right before reaching a junction with a playground ahead. Turn left at the junction to return to the main car park at the start.

Introduction:
Cooley Peninsula
and Slieve Gullion

The Cooley Peninsula is a mountainous finger of land sandwiched between Carlingford Lough and Dundalk Bay, extending for around 19km (11 miles) into the Irish Sea. At just over an hour's drive by car from either Belfast or Dublin, it features a diverse mix of landscape squeezed into an area of approximately 125km^2 – ranging from enchanting forests to broad green valleys, and from scenic stretches of coastline to high rugged peaks. Its highest mountain, Slieve Foye (588m/1,929ft), towers over Carlingford, a medieval town characterised by defensive walls, narrow lanes, tower houses and ruined castles. In the 12th century, the Norman lord Hugh de Lacy built an outpost castle on a strategic outcrop of rock overlooking Carlingford Lough. Before long, a settlement sprang up close to the castle. It was also a thriving fishing and trading port from the fourteenth to the sixteenth century.

Carlingford Lough (Loch Cairlinne, 'City of the Pool'), a U-shaped valley gouged out by glaciers during the ice age, is a sea inlet stretching along the length of the Cooley Peninsula on its northern end. The Irish playwright George Bernard Shaw once referred the area around Carlingford Lough as 'more beautiful than the Bay of Naples'. Originally named by the Vikings as *Kerlingfjordr*, meaning 'narrow sea inlet of the hag', it divides Northern Ireland to the north and the Republic of Ireland on the opposite side. Today, Carlingford Lough is a busy shipping haven, with ports at Warrenpoint and Greenore.

From high on the hills, the panorama of Carlingford Lough is as majestic as a Norwegian fjord, with a backdrop of mountains that sweep down to the sea. Two main ranges of hills extend north-west to south-east along the peninsula, separated by a deep gash at the Windy Gap. The Táin Way, a 40km (25-mile) long waymarked circuit winds around these hills and valleys. The trail, which begins and ends at Carlingford, is marked on the OSi Sheet 36 map and signposted on the ground by yellow arrows.

The Táin Way is the Cooley's testament to the epic tale of the Táin Bó Cúailgne (The Cattle Raid of Cooley), about the battle between Queen Maeve of Connacht and the hero Cúchulainn over the Brown Bull of Cooley.

North-west of the Cooley Peninsula is Slieve Gullion, the highest mountain in County Armagh. Its huge rounded mass dominates the local countryside, and sits in the epicentre of a ring of lower heather-covered hills. Slieve Gullion and these low-lying hills form part of a circular ring dyke volcano that erupted over 60 million years ago.

The Ring of Gullion is a unique geological landform in the British Isles, around 11km (6 miles) in diameter. It was the first ring dyke described in scientific literature and was named in 2014 as one of the top 100 geosites in Britain and Ireland. The ring dyke can be best appreciated from the summit of Slieve Gullion or Black Mountain on the Cooley Peninsula.

This section explores the hills and forests of the Cooley Peninsula – starting from the woodlands at Annaloughan, followed by Barnavave and Slieve Foye, the highest mountain in County Louth. The routes track their way inland, culminating in the classic viewpoint of the Flagstaff, before finishing on a circuit around Slieve Gullion. The table below lists, in order of height, Slieve Gullion and the nine other peaks on the Cooley Peninsula featured in this guidebook. Note: all heights are based on the OSi 1:50,000 Sheet 36 map.

Mountain Name	Height	Route
Slieve Foye	588m/1,929ft	22
Slieve Gullion	574m/1,883ft	26
The Eagles Rock	528m/1,732ft	23
Black Mountain/Clermont Cairn	508m/1,667ft	24
The Split Rock	457m/1,499ft	23
Clermont	444m/1,457ft	25
Anglesey Mountain	422m/1,385ft	25
The Ben Rock	410m/1,345ft	24
The Foxes Rock	404m/1,325ft	23
Barnavave	350m/1,148ft	21

Annaloughan Forest Loop

A straightforward walk on the slopes of Annaloughan Mountain and through the woods of Rockmarshall, which is popular with the locals.

Grade:	1
Distance:	8.5km (5¼ miles)
Ascent:	230m (755ft)
Time:	2½–3¼ hours
Map:	OSi 1:50,000 Sheet 36

Start/Finish: Car park at Fitzpatrick's Bar and Restaurant (www.fitzpatricks-restaurant.com) (**J 119**₉₉ **079**₂₆), which is open seven days a week and has a petting farm.

Getting there: From Dublin: exit the M1 at Junction 18; **from Belfast:** take the M1 exit just before Junction 18, toward Dundalk North/N52/Carlingford/R173/Ballymascanlan.

Once off the motorway, follow signs for the R173 in the direction of Greenore/Carlingford. Arrive at Fitzpatrick's Bar and Restaurant on the left after 7.2km (4½ miles), just before the junction for Ravensdale (R174).

This walk visits the site of a plane crash high on the slopes of Annaloughan Mountain. On 16 March 1942, a Liberator AL.577 drifted off course and crashed on the hillside, killing fifteen of the airmen on board (four survived). The plane had taken off from Egypt the day before en route to the United Kingdom. The aircraft had disobeyed orders to return to Egypt due to bad weather over the British Isles, resulting in the tragedy.

With the exception of the crash site, this loop walk of Annaloughan Mountain is signposted throughout with Purple Trail signage. One of the signs at the start of the route is hidden by foliage and is

Annaloughan Loop Walk signpost at Point A.

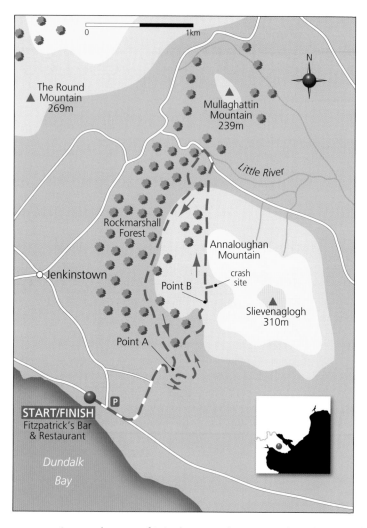

easy to miss, so take note of it in the route description. The uplands of Annaloughan Mountain are home to the perennial wildflower wood anemone (*Anemone nemorosa*), which forms a green carpet dotted with delicate, white-petalled flowers blossoming as early as spring. Pale-green lady fern (*Athyrium filix-femina*), with its feather-like texture, also forms in dense clumps on its higher slopes.

The trig-pillared hill of Slievenaglogh (310m/1,017ft) rises to the east of the crash site. On the map it looks near, and possibly an attractive top to ascend. However, the ground around it is extremely rough, boggy

Wreckage at the Liberator bomber crash site.

and riven with unseen holes and there are lengthy sections of barbed-wire fences barring the way. And so, this wee summit is omitted from this guidebook.

From the track along the fringes of Annaloughan Mountain, the trail veers into the dense forestry of Rockmarshall Wood, where pine and spruce trees dominate. The forest was once an estate woodland but the trees have since been felled and replanted over the years. This is a popular stretch with the locals, and chances are you will meet a good few of them!

Route Description

Exit the car park and turn left along the R173 in the direction of Carlingford. Cross a junction with care to reach a car park and lay-by on the left of the R173. Walk to the far end of the car park, then turn left onto a narrow road leading uphill.

Some houses dot the road after a bend as the road meanders further uphill. Although a Purple Trail signpost guides the way forward, keep your eyes peeled for a narrow, shaded footpath running alongside a high wall (grid ref: **J 125**26 **079**79). The footpath is located before a (right) bend at the top of the road, opposite Rockfield House. The Purple Trail signage is camouflaged by foliage here and can be easily missed.

The footpath swings around the wall to meet a gravel road. Turn right here, still following the Purple Trail. The road straightens after another bend and passes a mound of stones, a *cillín* or a burial ground for unbaptised children, on the right. The tarmac road soon gives way to a grassy track as it heads toward the forest.

Patch of bluebells in Annaloughan Forest.

Go right just after a barrier onto a path which links up with a broad forest track slightly higher. A clearing on the right reveals Dundalk Bay as the backdrop against the flat countryside.

Later, turn right onto a track that is lined with tall gorse bushes and continue for around 150m past a bend to reach a junction (grid ref: **J 127**₆₅ **080**₉₅, Point A). Turn right here onto a grassy track and head further uphill. The surrounding countryside, the ribbon of road and Dundalk Bay can be glimpsed through the pine trees.

The track is now flanked by conifer trees and soon goes round a bend to reach a T-junction. Turn right here, negotiate another bend, then finally reach a ladder stile at the edge of the woods.

Climb over the stile to meet a rising path that initially runs close to the woods. However, after crossing a small stream, the path later begins to veer away from the trees. At a Purple Trail signpost, the path splits into three (grid ref: **J 131**₀₄ **087**₅₀, Point B) – this is where a slight detour is needed to reach the crash site of the Liberator bomber.

The main path rises uphill to the left, and two subsidiary paths branch away to the right. Take the middle, narrower path, which soon crosses a small stream. The grassy path meanders around the base of a heathery knoll rising on your right. Flank the knoll, then veer left almost immediately and after just another few metres, reach the crash site of the Liberator bomber.

Some crash debris can be found on a flat grassy area here, and a plaque sits slightly further away (grid ref: **J 132**₂₁ **088**₆₁). When ready to leave, retrace steps back to Point B, then veer right to rejoin the Purple Trail.

The trail soon expands into a broad, stony track that runs along the edge of a forest. The track is also rocky along some sections but later dwindles to a narrow, earthen path flanked by a swathe of gorse. This is a fine stretch to take in the rough, surrounding countryside, with the rough summit of Slievenaglogh rising nearby to the east and Slieve Foye looming in the distance. Keep an eye out for the peregrine falcon (*Falco peregrinus*) that can sometimes be seen perched on fences or soaring at great speeds.

The path ends when it meets a metal ladder stile equipped with a handrail at a road. Climb over the stile, then turn left onto the road. After around 100m, a signpost for Annaloughan Loop Walk points toward the trees. Turn left here, cross a forest barrier, then follow a broad forest track through the dense Rockmarshall Forest. It is simply the case of following Purple Trail signposts until reaching a fork ahead, where you veer right to reach Point A once again.

Retrace steps from here back to the start.

Barnavave Loop from Carlingford

An easy, delightful half-day's excursion to one of the best viewpoints on the Cooley Peninsula.

Grade:	2
Distance:	8.5km (5¼ miles)
Ascent:	350m (1,148ft)
Time:	2¾–3½ hours
Map:	OSi 1:50,000 Sheet 36

Start/Finish: Car park at Carlingford tourist office at **J 189**₄₄ **116**₅₃.

Getting there: Carlingford may be approached by leaving the M1 at Junction 18 (if travelling from Dublin) or via Newry–Omeath (if travelling from Belfast). The tourist office is near the waterfront. **From Dublin:** Follow the R173/R175 in the direction of Carlingford. When approaching the village, turn left at the tourist office, following signs for 'Skypark' or 'Tourist Office', then immediately turn left again into the car park. **From Omeath:** soon after passing under the arch of King John's Castle in Carlingford, look out for the tourist office on the right. Turn right here, then immediately left into the car park.

The charming coastal village of Carlingford is dominated by its picturesque castle built by the Norman lord, Hugh de Lacy, in 1190. However, after King John of England reputedly spent the summer of 1210 in Carlingford, it was known henceforth as King John's Castle.

The initial part of this route weaves through the medieval streetscape of Carlingford, characterised by narrow lanes and old buildings. With the exception of a short off-the-beaten stretch on the summit of Barnavave (*Bearna Mhéabha*, 'Maeve's Gap'), all of the route is either on good paths, quiet country lanes or village roads. The initial part of the walk is marked by the Commons Loop but later the route follows Red Trail 'Barnavave Loop' signposts. The summit of Barnavave is the highlight of this walk, where glorious views of Carlingford Lough and Slieve Foye may be thoroughly enjoyed.

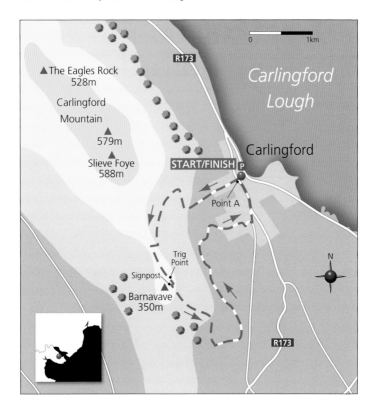

Route Description

Exit the car park with the tourist office on your right. Turn left onto the street, following Green/Blue/Red Trail signs on a lamp post to pass Taaffe's Castle, which was originally at the shoreline. The castle, built in the sixteenth century, was once the fortified residence of a rich merchant family. Slieve Foye can also be seen rising proudly above the woodlands behind the castle.

Reach a T-junction with a shop and Carlingford Post Office ahead. Turn left followed by a swift right a few metres ahead, following the main street. Continue past the Village Hotel and The Oystercatcher before reaching a junction of roads (Point A).

'Barnavave Loop Walk' is signposted on a metal post here and points toward a lane ahead. Head steeply up the lane following the signs, passing Carlingford Craft Shop then later a row of houses to reach a T-junction further uphill.

Leave the comfort of tarmac and continue uphill along a narrow path flanked by stone walls. The path is signposted 'Commons Loop' and later turns left at a gate before veering right to finally meet a ladder stile.

Climb over the stile, then immediately go right along a broad, grassy path flanked by gorse and bracken. Continue straight ahead at a cross-junction before reaching another one higher uphill. Leave the Commons Loop here by turning right on a path indicated by a Yellow Man signpost. Before long, an attractive panorama of Carlingford Lough, backed by the Mourne Mountains, and the coastline from Carlingford to Greenore opens up on the right.

The path soon reaches a Red Trail signpost at a bend, under the steep slopes of Slieve Foye. Head left here to continue on a broad path that meanders gradually uphill to reach a col. Signs diverge here; the Yellow Man points ahead whereas the Red Trail indicates left towards Barnavave.

Turn left in the direction of Barnavave and follow a grassy path that runs to the left of a fence. After around 150m, leave the path by veering left toward the spine of the spur and follow it until reaching the trig point of Barnavave (grid ref: **J 177**$_{96}$ **101**$_{49}$). This is a great viewpoint to admire the fierce-looking crags and gullies that line the steep southern face of Slieve Foye away to the north-west. To the left of Slieve Foye, green plains in the townlands of Ballygoly and Benagh extend westward, punctuated by the rounded shapes of Mullaghattin and Slievenaglogh in the distance. To the north and east, a glorious bird's-eye view along Carlingford Lough, backed by Slievemartin and the Mournes, completes the sublime vista.

For the purists, note that Barnavave has two tops. The trig point is on the northern top, and is slightly lower than the southern top, which is marked by Point 350m on the OSi map. The tops are separated by a narrow gap, and are around 135m apart. A wooden cross has been erected on the southern top by the local community and has been a tourist attraction since with thousands making the journey up.

From the trig point, continue ahead on a spur descending south-east (Carlingford Lough is now to your left) to reach two conspicuous medium-sized rocks. Take a sharp right here and a short, steep, grassy slope descends to a gap below. A signpost sits on the grassy gap, a useful marker in the mist. Veer left at the signpost and descend comfortably on a grassy path that runs to the left of a fence and some trees.

The path soon passes a large area of felled trees on the right. Dense pockets of bracken grow profusely on both sides of the path, sometimes completely obscuring it, especially over the summer season. An old stone wall is later met on the right and, from here, Red Trail signposts lead around a series of small switchbacks.

Not long after, cross a low gap in the wall, where the Red Trail signpost points right. A grassy path ambles gently downhill, crosses another low gap in the wall, then veers left to pass a ruined cottage. The path, now flanked by stone walls, soon reaches a set of signposts. The Rooskey (Purple Trail) Loop points ahead, whereas the Barnavave (Red Trail) Loop goes over yet another low gap in the wall.

Follow the Red Trail and finally climb over a ladder stile to reach a broad, gravel track. Once past a barrier, the track gets quite muddy and soon passes a cattle shed. Go left shortly at a fork and follow it around a bend to reach a road.

Follow the red arrows of the Barnavave Loop Walk and not the Yellow Man when signs diverge.

Turn left onto the road to pass some nice-looking country houses along the way. On clear days, the occupants of these houses must wake up to lovely ever-changing colours across Carlingford Lough, which sweeps away to the right.

After around 1.5km, the road takes a sharp right bend and weaves downhill toward Carlingford for around a kilometre to reach Dundalk Street. Turn left onto Dundalk Street to pass a church, school and the ruins of a Dominican friary before reaching a crossroads. Continue straight ahead at the crossroads, pass McAteer's Food House and finally reach the junction of roads once again at Point A.

Go right here and retrace steps back to the start.

The grassy path on the descent route runs to the left of a fence and an area of felled trees. It passes a ruined cottage after passing a low gap in the wall.

Slieve Foye Forest and Ridge Walk

This is the Cooley Peninsula at its best – a wooded trail, a rugged ridge, extensive views across Carlingford Lough and your chance to bag County Louth's highest peak!

Grade:	3
Distance:	10.5km (6½ miles)
Ascent:	585m (1,919ft)
Time:	4–5 hours, time added due to terrain
Map:	OSNI 1:50,000 Sheet 29 or OSi 1:50,000 Sheet 36

Start/Finish: Car park at Carlingford tourist office at **J 189**₄₄ **116**₅₃.
Getting there: As described in Route 21 (page 133).

At 588m/1,929ft, Slieve Foye is the highest mountain on the Cooley Peninsula and County Louth. Its summit offers dramatic views to the north and east of Carlingford Lough, with its majestic sweep of mountains in the background. The coastal towns of Rostrevor and Warrenpoint are tucked away at the northern end of Carlingford Lough, while its southern side is lined by the villages of Omeath, Carlingford and Greenore.

Carlingford Lough, which is actually a sea inlet rather than a lake, was once a long U-shaped valley. During the end of the ice age nearly 10,000 years ago, sea levels rose as the ice melted, drowned the valley and shaped the magnificent sea inlet on display today. The mouth of Carlingford Lough is dotted with tiny shingle islands, its shallow waters acting as a breeding ground for terns; its northern shores are made up of salt-marsh and mudflats, an ideal feeding area for the wintering Brent goose.

This route traverses the length of a hummocky ridge on Slieve Foye from the north-west to gain its summit. The bedrock on its rugged crest is a combination of granite, dolerite and gabbro formed during the Palaeogene period around 40 million years ago. Gabbro, a coarse-grained dark-coloured igneous rock, has magnetic properties and has been known to interfere with compass needles. Take heed in the mist, or reserve this walk for a clear day, where you should encounter no difficulties and at the same time enjoy the wide-ranging and spectacular views that are on offer.

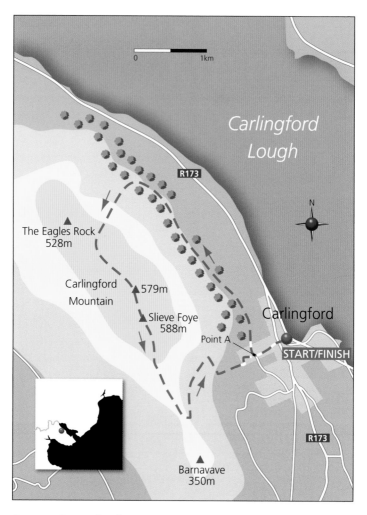

Route Description

Exit the car park with the tourist office on your right. Turn left onto the street, following Green/Blue/Red Trail signs on a lamp post to pass Taaffe's Castle, which was originally at the shoreline. The castle, built in the sixteenth century, was once the fortified residence of a rich merchant family. Slieve Foye can be seen rising proudly above the woodlands behind the castle.

Reach a T-junction with a shop and Carlingford Post Office ahead. Turn left followed by a swift right a few metres ahead, following the main street. Continue past the Village Hotel and The Oystercatcher before reaching a

Blue/Red Trail arrows and Yellow Man signage at the start of the walk.

junction of roads. 'Barnavave Loop Walk' is signposted on a metal post here and points toward a lane ahead. Head steeply up the lane following the signs, passing Carlingford Craft Shop, then later a row of houses to reach a T-junction further uphill (Point A).

Turn right here onto a track flanked by stone walls and fences, following Yellow Man or Blue/Red Trail signs. Continue to reach a metal gate near a forest then follow a gravel track gradually uphill until it forks. An attractive panorama of Carlingford Lough, with its backdrop of mountains, opens up to the right over this stretch.

Veer left at the fork, still following the signposts, and not long after, the trail passes a zip line adventure centre on the left. The track here is flanked by a rich plantation of pine trees and soon crosses the Golden River Bridge. Lovely cascades topple down rocky, bracken-covered slopes to the left of the bridge.

Continue along the track for another 1.7km to reach a tarmac road soon after crossing a forest barrier. Veer left on the road, which sits at the bottom of a bend, and go a short distance uphill to reach a car park equipped with picnic tables.

The rugged hillside now rises away to the left (south-west) of the car park. Aim for a green metal stile at a fence and ascend the grassy, and at times soggy, slope beyond. As the slope steepens, zigzag on grassy ramps among the rocky outcrops and slabs. Finally, bypass a large outcrop of rock on the right to reach the top of the ridge of Slieve Foye.

Veer left along the ridge, which extends in a north-west to south-east direction. It looks relatively straightforward on the map but in reality, it is anything but that. The terrain along the ridge is entertainingly rugged, hummocky and full of rocky outcrops – take care in mist. Head south-east as the ground rises to Point 579m before undulating to reach a trig pillar perched on a rocky outcrop marking the summit of Slieve Foye (grid ref: **J 169**04 **119**33).

The summit area is scattered with rocks and slabs of various shapes and sizes. The surrounding view is stupendous! Look back the way you came along the ridge to appreciate its rough and complex character.

Golden River Bridge in Slieve Foye woods.

Green plains fed by the Big River and Little River lie to the west, backed by the rounded, brown humps of Mullaghattin and Slievenaglogh. A broad ridge of low-lying hills extends north-westward from there to Black Mountain. However, the most impressive views are away to the north and east, along Carlingford Lough, which extends for miles from Warrenpoint to Ballagan Point, and backed by the scenic Rostrevor hills and the higher Mourne range farther away.

The descent route off the summit needs care, especially in the mist. Begin by descending south-east on a vague path for around 200m, bypassing any rocky outcrops if needed, then later veer southward down a steep spur. Try not to drift too far from the spine of the spur and follow the path to reach the top of a steep, grassy gully flanked by rocky outcrops (grid ref: **J 170**₉₉ **116**₂₇). A black-and-white post marks the top of the gully.

Do not attempt to enter or descend the gully at any cost, but instead flank it on the right. Locate a path signposted by purple arrows, which weaves its way down grassy ramps, past some large rocky outcrops. As the steepness relents, the spur changes direction to roughly south-east. Now an obvious path, still signposted by purple arrows, leads to a broad col below. Slieve Foye's lower neighbour, Barnavave can also be seen further ahead beyond the col.

Turn left at the col onto a gravel path signposted by Yellow Man signs. The broad path leads comfortably downhill, soon passing under the steep, craggy slopes of Slieve Foye. After a large switchback, the path reaches a junction (grid ref: **J 179**77 **111**87) where a signpost for the Commons/Slieve Foye Loop points ahead.

Veer left downhill here onto a broad, grassy path flanked by gorse and bracken to reach a metal gate by a fence further below. You are now actually doing the Commons Loop in reverse back to Carlingford! Veer left and climb over a ladder stile there to meet a narrow, gravel path flanked by bracken-covered stone walls.

Follow the path around a bend to reach a gate. Go through the gate and keep following the path which finally leads back to the junction at Point A. Retrace steps from here back to the start.

The stunning view across Carlingford Lough to Rostrevor and the Mourne Mountains from high on Slieve Foye.

The Eagles Rock to The Foxes Rock from Greer's Quay

A wild walk along a line of quiet, rugged hills north-west of Slieve Foye.	**Grade:**	3
	Distance:	11.5km (7¼ miles)
	Ascent:	655m (2,149ft)
	Time:	4–5 hours
	Map:	OSNI 1:50,000 Sheet 29 or OSi 1:50,000 Sheet 36

Start/Finish: Greer's Quay (grid ref: **J 156**₅₄ **151**₂₁).

Getting there: From Carlingford: drive along the R173 for 5km (3 miles) towards Omeath. Leave the road and turn right into Greer's Quay (it is signposted) around a kilometre after passing the entrance for Slieve Foye Woods. Park in the small car park on the right at the quay. There are spaces for around four to five cars. **From Omeath:** drive towards Carlingford. Greer's Quay is located approximately 2.5km (1½ miles) after Omeath on the left.

Note: a section of the Táin Way at the start of the walk is closed annually on 23 December, and this is also signposted along the route.

Greer's Quay, built to help develop Carlingford Lough's fishing industry, was named after a local nineteenth-century landlord. Its car park near the shoreline offers panoramic views across the waters of Carlingford Lough toward Slievemartin. The Great Eastern Greenway, a 7km (4¼-mile) waymarked walking trail, runs along the shoreline passing through here. Built mostly on a former railway line, the trail connects Omeath and Carlingford, running though fields, over bridges and old level crossings, all the time hugging the shore.

The core of this walk traces a line over a rugged range of hills high above Ballyonan. For the uninitiated, it is an eye-opener to the wild nature of the landscape that extends westward from the Eagles Rock to the Foxes Rock. The latter lies above the Windy Gap, which was formed by erosion

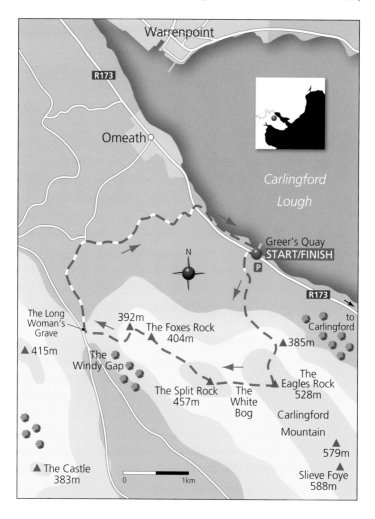

along a geological fault of the Carlingford Complex around 60 million years ago. The fault brought together two different rock types. The craggy, black rocks to the east of the Windy Gap, and on to Slieve Foye, are gabbro – a rock containing magnetic minerals that are said to interfere with compass needles. The grassier, rounded hills to the west and south-west of the gap have a bedrock of granite, a light-coloured igneous rock.

Looking east-south-east towards the ridge from Eagles Rock to Slieve Foye from the Split Rock.

Route Description

From Greer's Quay, head back out to the R173 and turn right in the direction of Omeath. Exercise due caution while walking along the side of the road, even for a short distance, as it can get quite busy. Cross the road after around 100m to reach a metal gate with a ladder stile by a signpost for the Táin Way.

Climb over the stile and follow a broad, grassy path for around 300m to reach a bend. Soon after the bend, the path passes a house sheltered by a copse of trees away to the left. Turn right after crossing a stream and continue until meeting a metal ladder stile by a wall.

Follow a broad, grassy path signposted by Yellow Man signs beyond the stile. After crossing a gap in the wall, leave the path and ascend a grassy slope. Flank a patch of scree to the right and follow a stream up the moderately steep slope to reach a hollow due south of Point 385m.

On 12 December 1996, a Sikorsky S-76B helicopter en route to Ballyedmond crashed as it made its descent to Warrenpoint, killing all three on board. Some crash debris can still be found on the slopes here at Ballyonan, so keep a look out as you climb.

At the hollow, veer south-west and ascend a steep slope, zigzagging along grassy ramps between large slabs of rock. The slope veers south, then south-east towards Eagles Rock. Finally, outflank a rocky crag to the left to reach the ridgetop. Carlingford Lough, backed by the Rostrevor hills and Mourne Mountains, sweeps eastward below, extending from Warrenpoint toward Greenore. The Newry River can also be seen winding away to the north-west.

A large, vertiginous, rocky crag sits impressively on top of the ridge – this is not the summit but perhaps the 'actual' Eagles Rock. You may choose to climb some rock steps to the top of this lofty crag, but if not, veer left and continue south-east along the ridge.

Another rather large outcrop of rock with a low overhang on the Carlingford (eastern) side is soon reached. The roofed, rocky shelter under this overhang makes a fine lunch spot. If you choose not to stop here for lunch, veer right of the outcrop and continue slightly further to reach the rocky, unmarked summit of the Eagles Rock (grid ref: **J 158**58 **132**03).

Descend westward from the summit in the direction of a broad and boggy col known as the White Bog. The ground

The Split Rock, around 100m away from the summit.

is rough, but aim due north of two small tarns below, then continue westward from here up a moderately steep slope to reach a pile of rocks on the summit of the Split Rock (grid ref: **J 148**79 **131**92).

Gaze eastward from here back towards Eagles Rock and trace your eye along the hummocky ridge extending to Slieve Foye to appreciate the wild character of the barren landscape. The rough hillside of Ballinteskin and Ballyonan can also be seen to the north from here.

Strangely enough, if you walk just 100m further from the summit, you will come across a distinct cleft in an outcrop of rock (grid ref: **J 147**86 **132**10) with a capstone on top – could this be the actual 'split rock' that the name of the summit refers to?

Next, head north-west down to the next col before continuing uphill to cross two fences before reaching a cairn on a rocky slab marking the summit of the Foxes Rock (grid ref: **J 140**29 **138**63). Summit views of the surrounding landscape are just as desolate and wild from here.

A short, broad ridge connects the Foxes Rock with its subsidiary top, Point 392m. Here, turn left and descend south, then south-west toward a forest below. Pick up an informal, grassy track which soon veers away from the trees to reach a metal ladder stile and a low stile at a fence (grid ref: **J 131**37 **138**80) below.

A track beyond the stile leads to a car park at the Long Woman's Grave, tucked in a narrow hollow known as the Windy Gap. Legend has it that it is the grave of a Spanish noblewoman who married Lorcan, the younger son of the chieftain of Omeath. On his passing, the chieftain willed his lands be divided between his two sons, Conn Óg and Lorcan. Conn Óg

145

tricked his brother by bringing him here, with the promise of land as far as the eye could see. However, the barren surroundings were Lorcan's only inheritance. Fortunately, Lorcan owned a ship, began trading in the east and became wealthy. During a trip to Cadiz, he saved the lives of a Spanish aristocrat and his 7ft-tall daughter, Cauthleen. They fell in love and returned to Omeath where he took her back to the Windy Gap. On seeing the bleakness of the land, Cauthleen collapsed and died. The heartbroken Lorcan at once threw himself into a bog here and drowned. His body was never discovered, but it is said Cauthleen's body was found and buried where she lay. Today, the Long Woman's Grave is marked by large rocks at the car park.

When ready, turn right out of the car park and walk along the road in the direction of Newry, later turning right at a junction towards Omeath. The road now dips quite steeply. After around 1.5km, turn sharply right onto a narrow road just after a Yellow Man sign.

Cross a concrete bridge over a river, following the road that meanders along the quiet countryside, passing a handful of houses and the green, cultivated fields of Ballinteskin. There are lovely faraway views of Warrenpoint to the left, with Rostrevor peeping ahead.

After some sharp bends, the road meets the R173. Cross the R173 and take a broad path leading onto the Greenway at a bridge on its opposite end.

Turn right along the broad footpath of the Greenway and walk south-east, with Carlingford Lough now away to your left. Pass the Calvary Shrine and the grounds of the former Táin Holiday Village before reaching Greer's Quay once again.

The view south-east from the Foxes Rock towards the Split Rock, at sunset.

The Hills and Forest of Ravensdale

A scenic circuit of a low-lying ridge and beautiful woodlands through one of the Cooley Peninsula's loveliest valleys.

Grade:	3
Distance:	16km (10 miles)
Ascent:	565m (1,854ft)
Time:	5–6 hours
Map:	OSNI 1:50,000 Sheet 29 or OSi 1:50,000 Sheet 36

Start/Finish: Car park at rear of Lumper's Bar (**J 100**₄₅ **108**₀₅), €3 charge to park. If you have access to two cars, leave the second car along the L30906 on a small lay-by (grid ref: **J 091**₀₀ **132**₅₀) on the right before a junction. There are spaces for three to four cars. This reduces the length of the walk by 3km (45 minutes to 1 hour) at the start.

Getting there: From Dublin: Leave the M1 at Junction 18 for Dundalk North/Carlingford/R173/Ballymascanlan. At the roundabout, take the fourth exit onto the N52. At the next roundabout, take the first exit onto the R132. After around 350m, reach another small roundabout, take the first exit and stay on the R132. After around 4.2km (2½ miles), the road veers right to reach a T-junction. Turn right there onto the R174. Continue for just under 4.5km (2¾ miles) along Ravensdale to reach Lumper's Bar.

From Belfast: At Junction 19, exit towards Ravensdale/R174. Continue to a T-junction and turn right onto the R174. Continue for just under 4.5km (2¾ miles) along Ravensdale to reach Lumper's Bar.

Ravensdale is a picturesque valley running for some 6km (3¾ miles) in a quiet nook of the Cooley Peninsula. It is bordered on the west by the Flurry River, whose waters turned the wheels of several mills in the nineteenth century. At the time, there were mills along its banks for linen bleaching, grinding flax, corn, oatmeal and flour, and for the manufacture of edge tools.

Geologically, Ravensdale is part of the Slieve Gullion ring dyke. Both the long-distance waymarked trails of the Táin Way and Ring of Gullion Way also pass through the valley. The wooded valley, which reveals its finest colours in autumn, was shaped by ice during the last glaciation over

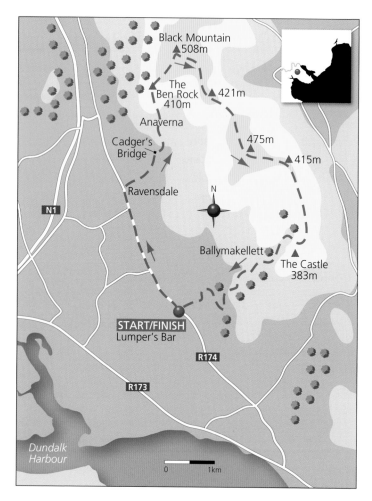

10,000 years ago. The area around Ravensdale was also once a demesne of the Baron Clermont, who built an austere-looking Victorian house in the area around the 1840s, complete with a lofty campanile with an open belvedere atop. The mansion was sold three times before being burnt in 1921 during the emergence of the Irish Free State.

This route passes through a scenic stretch of the R174 along the base of Ravensdale before heading up the highest top in the area, Black Mountain or Clermont Cairn, named after the demesne owners of old. The next part of the walk undulates across a low-lying ridge giving good views to the east and west, and extending some 5.5km (3½ miles) to Slievetrasna. The waymarked descent follows a section of the Táin Way through the

Approaching Black Mountain/Clermont Cairn, with its summit masts ahead.

beautifully wooded area of Ballymakellett, a comfortable way to round up the circuit around Ravensdale.

Route Description

Turn right out of Lumper's car park and walk northward along the R174 for around 2.75km. Pass a cemetery, school and church before reaching a disused building, which was once a post office, on the left. Continue along the road a short distance after the former post office to reach a lane (L30906) on the right.

Walk up the lane and pass a small lay-by on the right after around 250m. The lane forks soon after, with signs for Caraban Mass Rock (indicating right) and Anaverna Mountain (pointing left). It is said that the Mass rock was where Saint Oliver Plunkett once celebrated the Eucharist during penal times.

Take the right fork and continue uphill for around 350m to reach a bend. Leave the lane here and veer left to cross a small concrete bridge over a tiny stream. Follow a gravel path, which soon turns grassy, to the right of a river to reach Cadger's Bridge (grid ref: **J 094**81 **137**35). This path was an old access route, named after herring sellers who used to bring their catch over the mountains to Dundalk market.

Go through a metal gate here, then proceed uphill on a broad, grassy track. The track is flanked by drystone-walled fields to the left and a river-filled ravine away to your right. The greenish-brown hillside of Anaverna and rounded lump of the Ben Rock can also be seen rising to the left. Later the track veers left to reach some standing stones on a grassy shoulder (grid ref: **J 096**35 **145**36). This is where the annual All-Ireland *Poc Fada* (Irish for 'long puck') starts. In the competition, which began in 1960, the participants puck a *sliotar* with a hurley over a course of around 5km (3 miles).

From the standing stones, ascend a moderately steep slope of grass and heather to reach the pointed summit of the Ben Rock. A low wall snakes to the north-east from here. Follow the wall (to its right) at first, but later veer (left) away from it to ascend an indistinct, boggy track to reach the summit of Black Mountain/Clermont Cairn (grid ref: **J 099**₁₁ **157**₅₂).

The summit is decorated with transmission masts, but all-round views are good, especially across the Aghadavoyle Valley to Slieve Gullion, with one half of the roughly circular ring dyke of the Ring of Gullion fairly obvious. The panorama includes the Warrenpoint coastline, Carlingford Lough and the hills above Rostrevor farther away to the east.

When ready, follow a broad, undulating ridge to the south-east from the summit. A broad track with boggy sections leads to a small cairn with a wooden post at Point 421m. From there, descend eastward down to a broad col, before ascending to Point 475m, which is marked by a large summit cairn with a circular shelter (grid ref: **J 112**₈₄ **139**₁₄). There are good views here toward the hummocky ridge of Slieve Foye roughly south-eastwards, Carlingford Lough again to the east and also of the vast plains westward.

Next, descend roughly eastward toward Point 415m. Underfoot conditions are quite rough initially, but improve on reaching a broad track, where a raised boardwalk helps avoid boggy sections. The track soon passes a Táin Way (Yellow Man) signpost on the left. Ignore that and continue descending along the spur until the track veers close to a fence to reach the corner of a forest (grid ref: **J 124**₁₉ **120**₅₈).

Turn right here onto a gravel path indicated by another Yellow Man signpost. The path runs close to the fence to reach a metal ladder stile. Climb over the stile and continue on a path through the trees to emerge onto a broad, gravel track. Turn left there and follow the track which runs along the forest edge to your left.

Veer right on reaching a junction with a Yellow Man signpost to follow a track flanked by conifers and gorse. Later at a T-junction, turn right and follow the track downhill to reach a clearing giving fine views of the countryside and hills above Ravensdale. The masts on Clermont Cairn also protrude in the distance.

Turn right at the next T-junction to pass a beautiful, wooded forest before reaching a barrier at the forest entrance. Turn left at a road after the barrier and follow it around a bend. A straight stretch then meanders past some houses to finally reach the car park at Lumper's Bar once again.

Ballymakellett Forest.

150

Anglesey Mountain, Clermont and Flagstaff

A circuit along the northern fringes of Cooley that culminates in a classic viewpoint of the peninsula.

Grade:	3
Distance:	12km (7½ miles)
Ascent:	480m (1,575ft)
Time:	3¾–4¾ hours
Map:	OSNI 1:50,000 Sheet 29 or OSi 1:50,000 Sheet 36

Start/Finish: Car park off the main Newry–Omeath road at Cornamucklagh House (formerly known as Davey's, grid ref: **J 121**22 **190**62). Cornamucklagh House is open seven days a week, serving food in the evening from Thursday to Sunday. Alternatively, you may park at Flagstaff Viewpoint (grid ref: **J 106**03 **202**00) and do the upper portion of the route from there, omitting Fathom Forest altogether.

Getting there: Coming from Dublin or Belfast, leave the M1/A1 and take the B113 exit towards A2/Newry. At the roundabout, take the Dublin Road exit (second exit coming from Dublin, first exit coming from Belfast) in the direction of Newry. After approximately 2km (1¼ miles) take a sharp right turn into Drumalane Road at the church, following signs for Omeath/Greenore (B79). Continue for around 8km (5 miles) along the road to reach Cornamucklagh House. Leave the main road there, turning right into the car park at Cornamucklagh House.

'If I could only be as a rowan-berry on Fathom Hill'
– Séamas Mór Mac Mhurchaidh (1720–50)

Fathom (from *Feadán*, a stream or watercourse) Forest was a favourite haunt of rapparee and poet Séamas Mór Mac Mhurchaidh until he was arrested and hanged in Armagh in 1750. Its slopes rise steeply from the roadside on the eastern end, close to the Newry River. The forest – where the song of the chiffchaff and robin can be heard – has a lush cover of birch, larch and tall pine trees. This route takes us up and down the beautiful forested slopes of Fathom, then over two low-lying hills south

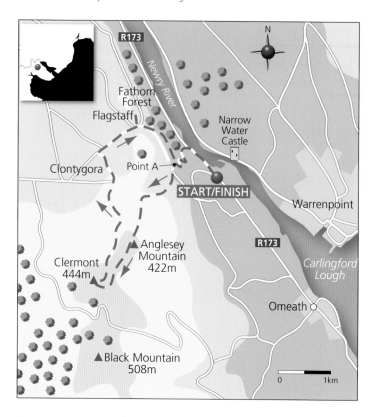

Narrow Water Castle seen across the Newry River, at the start of the walk.

of the Ring of Gullion Way. The isolated tops of Anglesey Mountain and Clermont are the two northernmost summits over 400m on the Cooley Peninsula, and are normally quiet compared to the main range of Slieve Foye and Black Mountain to the south.

The descent route takes us into the townland of Clontygora (*Chluainte Gabhra*, 'meadow of the goats'), passing a court tomb built by Neolithic farmers around 3500 BC. Known locally as the 'King's Ring', this court tomb, unusually, faces north and not east towards the sun. Today, all that remains is just an arrangement of tall stones, some over 2m (6.5ft) in height. The original structure was more extensive and consisted of a deep, enclosed U-shaped forecourt, guarded by two large portal stones, and three burial chambers. The first chamber is the widest, with tall granite boulders supported by large roof slabs and a capstone.

The highlight of the route is the Flagstaff viewpoint near the end. Flagstaff was named from the custom of raising a flag to signal the approach of ships navigating the waters of Carlingford Lough. This is one of the classic viewpoints on the Cooley Peninsula, giving stupendous views along the Newry River and Carlingford Lough. The viewpoint, which comes complete with a large car park and picnic tables, can get quite busy during the summer. If parking here, it is advisable to keep all valuables and belongings out of sight in your vehicle, as break-ins to parked cars are, sadly, a common occurrence.

Route Description

Cross the main road at Cornamucklagh House, then turn left and walk in the direction of Newry. There is a soft verge of sorts – nevertheless, take care as it is a busy road. After around 250m, as the soft verge begins to peter out, reach a lay-by on the right at a 'County Louth/Ireland's Ancient East' signboard.

Leave the main road here and go right onto a narrow, grassy path. The intermittent path runs along an old dismantled railway track and meanders close to the Newry River. It soon passes the County Bridge, which straddles the road away to the left, on the border between Northern Ireland and the Republic of Ireland. Narrow Water Castle can also be seen on the opposite bank of the river away to the right. Built in 1560, the castle once defended the entrance to the Newry River estuary.

The path, now flanked by gorse, soon reaches a copse of trees slightly further along. Head left now to cross a low fence and meet the main road again. Cross the road with care, then turn right and walk on the soft verge, in the direction of Newry. Pass a 'Ring of Gullion' signboard, a large landscaped house, a small lane, and finally after around 250m, another house on the left.

Leave the main road here (grid ref: **J 115**31 **196**55) and turn left onto a tarmac lane immediately after the house. After yet another house on the

Looking south-east to Slieve Foye from Anglesey Mountain, with Carlingford Lough to the left.

left, the tarmac soon gives way to a muddy, broad track as it enters Fathom Forest. Ignore all subsidiary tracks and continue steadily uphill for around 250m to reach a prominent bend. Veer right at the bend to pass a forest barrier soon and reach a junction. Turn left here and follow the track as it weaves up the forest in a series of switchbacks. As the track begins to flatten over a straight stretch, look out on the left for a narrow, grassy path (grid ref: **J 113**₄₅ **193**₅₅ – Point A).

Turn left here onto the holly-lined path and follow it gradually uphill to emerge out of the trees on Ferryhill Road above. Turn left onto the road and follow it for around 150m to meet a lay-by at a forest entrance. Go right, into the forest, following a path for around 300m to reach a clearing just before a boulder (grid ref: **J 112**₄₄ **189**₂₇). Then turn left here towards a gate at the forest boundary.

Go through the gate, veer right and follow the edge of some trees uphill – south-west initially then later due west – to reach a fence at the base of a moderately steep slope leading up to Anglesey Mountain. Head up the grassy and heathery slope using an informal path running to the left of the fence. The gradient relents nearer the top on a summit area consisting of mainly heather and some scattered rocks.

The actual top of Anglesey Mountain is unmarked but there is a cairn (grid ref: **J 106**₀₉ **178**₃₁) just off the summit overlooking Carlingford Lough. The views are extensive from here and include the plains fed by the Ryland River to the south-east and Carlingford Lough, which is flanked by the forested slopes of Slievemartin and Slieve Foye.

From Anglesey Mountain, follow a fence and descend south-west to a col below. Go up the next rise and keep following the fence as it veers right toward the unmarked, grassy top of Clermont (grid ref: **J 098**₄₀ **171**₃₆). The actual top sits above a slight rise just after a stile at the fence. Black

Mountain or Clermont Cairn rises to the south, and the road leading up to its transmission masts can be clearly seen from here.

Retrace steps back to the stile at the fence from Clermont. Cross the wobbly stile with care, then descend northward on trackless moorland, aiming for the corner of a forest below. Anglesey Mountain is a good landmark to ensure you are heading in the desired direction, and it now rises prominently away to your right as you descend.

At the corner of the forest, keep the trees on your left and follow the forest boundary for around 250m to its other end. Here, step up onto a broad, distinct track and go left, following it downhill to reach the corner of a fence. Turn left here onto a broad, grassy track, passing through several metal gates, to finally meet a road.

Turn right onto Upper Ferryhill Road, ignore all junctions and follow it downhill to reach Clontygora Court Tomb on the left (grid ref: **J 098**78 **194**33). This 3500 BC burial site and its façade of tall stones is worth taking a detour to visit. When ready, continue along the road to reach a T-junction.

Clontygora Court Tomb.

Turn right here onto Sloan Road and, before long, arrive at the entrance for the Flagstaff viewpoint.

Leave the road here and walk up to its car park, then onto its viewpoint (grid ref: **J 106**03 **202**48), which looks down on Fathom Forest. The panoramic vista from here to the south-east is one of the finest in the area – dominated by Carlingford Lough, whose Mediterranean-blue waters are guarded by the green, forested slopes of Slievemartin on one end and the brown, menacing face of Slieve Foye at the other. Down on the estuary, Narrow Water Castle stands watch near the mouth of the Newry River. A ribbon of road can also be seen snaking towards the white and grey concrete jumble of Warrenpoint, which glistens in the sun.

Retrace steps from the Flagstaff viewpoint back to the road. Veer left here, ignore the first junction on the left and continue along the road. Just after the end of some trees on the right, leave the road and go left to cross a forest barrier onto a track beyond (grid ref: **J 107**77 **199**90). The track leads into Fathom Forest. After around 200m, leave the track at a bend and continue ahead along a narrow, leafy, gravel path through the trees. The path arrives at Point A once again and from here, retrace your steps down the forest back to the start.

Slieve Gullion

An enjoyable circuit of the highest mountain in County Armagh.	**Grade:**	3
	Distance:	14.5km (9 miles)
	Ascent:	440m (1,444ft)
	Time:	4½–5½ hours
	Map:	OSNI 1:50,000 Sheet 29

Start/Finish: Slieve Gullion Forest Park car park at **J 040**98 **197**63.

Getting there: Coming from Dublin or Belfast, leave the M1/A1 and take the B113 exit towards Forkhill/Newry South. Follow signs for Forkhill or Slieve Guillion Forest Park at the roundabout. Follow the B113 for around 6.5km (4 miles) before turning right into the forest park. Follow the road into the courtyard to reach a large car park with ample spaces.

Slieve Gullion Forest Park has a visitor information centre, café, picnic tables, woodland trails, colour-coded running trails, an ornamental walled garden and an Adventure Playpark which includes a zip line, slides, climbing frames and a specially designed toddlers' area. The closing time of the car park is displayed on a sign and this varies every month over the year.

At 573m/1,880ft, Slieve Gullion (*Sliabh gCuillinn*, 'mountain of the steep slope') is the highest mountain in County Armagh and on the Ring of Gullion. It is a solitary mountain, shaped by glaciation and surrounded by a number of low-lying hills: Sturgan Mountain (250m/820ft) and Camlough Mountain (423m/1,388ft) separated by Cam Lough to the north; Tievecrom (283m/928ft) and Croslieve (308m/1,011ft) to the south; and Aughanduff (234m/768ft) to the north-west.

The huge mass of Slieve Gullion itself is ancient – the remnant of a Paleocene volcanic complex encircled by a 60 million-year-old ring dyke that has attracted many geologists from around the world. The ring dyke, which is around 11km (7 miles) in diameter, was formed due to the collapse of the surface above a retreating chamber of molten rock.

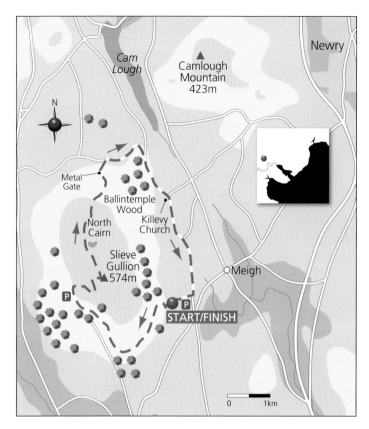

There are two cairns on its large summit plateau: one just north of a tiny mountain lake, and a larger circular one on its southern end. The 4m (13ft) high southern cairn of Slieve Gullion has a kerb of large stones around its perimeter, which measures around 30m/98ft in diameter. The large cairn is also a Neolithic passage tomb, the highest surviving one in Ireland. Its entrance is aligned with the setting sun of the winter solstice. Back in 1789, the chamber was opened by a group of tomb raiders searching for the old hag Calliagh Berra, but only a few human bones were found.

Route Description

Exit the car park and pick up the Slieve Gullion Forest Drive that heads uphill via a series of switchbacks. The tarmac road passes under a lush canopy of trees including the Lodgepole pine, Sitka spruce, Japanese larch and Scots pine – if you're lucky, you might even spot the odd red squirrel or the elusive pine marten.

Slieve Gullion from the east.

The road soon contours along the southern slopes of Slieve Gullion to reach an upper car park (grid ref: **J 018**30 **200**00) complete with picnic tables. Given the expansive views of the low-lying hills and plains to the south, it is hardly surprising this car park is popular with the locals. There are also information panels outlining the geology of the area and information on the Ring of Gullion Way.

Walk to the opposite end of the car park and continue for around 50m to meet a distinct path on the right. Leave the road here and go right onto a path made up of concrete steps. Pass through a swinging wooden gate at a fence and follow the path as it zigzags uphill, until it swings around the southern slopes of Slieve Gullion to reach a stone shelter (grid ref: **J 022**20 **200**14). Dundalk Bay now stretches to the south-east and a wide expanse of green agricultural plains , which is punctuated by low brown hills, extends to the south-west.

Sizeable steps made up of large rocks and boulders are installed along sections to prevent further erosion to the hillside. The going gets moderately steep as the path swings north, then east, at which point

Orientation plaque on the cairn on Slieve Gullion's summit.

158

Looking eastward to the Mourne Mountains and Cooley Peninsula from Slieve Gullion's North Cairn.

the length of the Cooley Peninsula comes into view, with the mast on Clermont Cairn and the hummocky ridge of Slieve Foye prominent. Soon the large cairn on the summit of Slieve Gullion appears. Steep rocky steps lead to the summit which consists of a large burial chamber, trig point and a smaller, beehive cairn (grid ref: **J 024**79 **203**28).

There is an orientation plate on the cairn, making identification of landmarks both near and afar fun (see if you can spot all of them!). The surrounding views are all-encompassing from here and include the Ring of Gullion, Armagh drumlins, the mountains of Mourne and the Cooley Peninsula. On a clear day, even the Antrim hills and Wicklow Mountains can be discerned on the distant horizon.

From the summit cairn, try and pick out the tiny Calliagh Berra's Lough on the plateau around 600m away to the north-west. The lough is named after the old hag Cailleach Beara, who, according to legend, in her altered form of a beautiful young woman, once tricked the mythical warrior-hunter Fionn Mac Cumhaill. The story finds Fionn retrieving the woman's golden ring from the lake, only to emerge from its waters to find an old, wrinkled hag cackling. There and then, Fionn was transformed to a weak, unrecognisable old man. However, on his return from the mountain, Fionn's loyal hounds smelt him and knew he was their master. The Fianna and the hounds hunted the hag and forced her to restore Fionn to his youth, but unfortunately his hair remained permanently white. So take heed, as it is said this fate also befalls anyone who swims in this lake!

Some rocky steps lead north-west from the summit toward Calliagh Berra's Lough. Before long, the ground turns peaty on an intermittent path which becomes increasingly boggy and eroded. Move towards the edge of the plateau onto drier ground if it gets too boggy, especially on or after a wet day. An intermittent path meanders along to the left of the lake, leading to the North Cairn of Slieve Gullion (grid ref: **J 021**15 **211**25), a multiple cist cairn dating back to the Bronze Age (2500–1500 BC).

From the North Cairn, walk north-east along a broad, distinct but eroded path that is rocky in places. Cam Lough ('crooked lake') and its namesake mountain can now be seen ahead. The lake, the largest in the area, takes its name from its irregular shape. On a clear day, the peaks of Mourne can be seen farther away, with Slieve Donard standing head and shoulders above the rest.

The descending path turns grassier and soon broadens as Ballintemple Wood comes into view. Go through a metal gate at a fence (grid ref: **J 024**51 **226**36) and continue, to reach another metal gate around 350m away at Ballard Road. A farmhouse sits opposite the road beyond the gate. Turn right onto the road and follow it as it descends via a series of switchbacks. It passes a roadside viewpoint on the left (blocked by large boulders at the time of writing), giving fine views of the stretch of countryside dominated by green fields and dotted with houses. These farmlands, populated with sheep and cattle, are divided into strips of rectangular fields partitioned by drystone walls, hedges and banks of earth.

Ignore a junction on the left at a 'Give Way' sign and continue along Ballintemple Road. The road meanders below Ballintemple Wood and soon reaches a junction on the left with a sign for St Moninna's Well. Ignore the junction and continue ahead, along a section of the Ring of Gullion and the Ulster Way. The ruins and cemetery of Killevy Church, dating from the tenth century, are soon passed on the right. Killevy is the site of Ireland's most important early convent, founded by St Moninna in the fifth century. St Monnina, who is buried in the churchyard, is also the patron saint of Killevy.

Pass some elegant country houses and follow the road for another 2.5km, ignoring two junctions on the left. On reaching a crossroads, turn right into Wood Road, still following signs for the Ring of Gullion and the Ulster Way. Finally, take a left at Annahaia Cottage, followed by a right at a fork soon after.

Now, simply follow the road uphill to reach the car park at the start.